Letter from the Editor

Dear Readers,

We are very excited to welcome you all to the fifth volume of The Arbitration Brief. The Arbitration Brief is a student publication of the American University Washington College of Law. The Arbitration Brief aims to become a leading academic publication for arbitration-related matters in the United States and abroad.

The Arbitration Brief is an entirely student-run organization. We publish articles submitted by professors, arbitrators, practitioners, and students alike. All articles are selected, edited, and published by the Brief's editorial board and staff. We are particularly excited to publish this issue as it is the first publication since The Arbitration Brief went out of circulation in 2014.

The Arbitration Brief would like to thank the authors of this issue for their patience, responsiveness, and cooperation with our editorial board as we revised their articles. The Arbitration Brief staff would like to also specially acknowledge Professor Horacio Grigera-Naón, Dr. Björn Arp, Professor Padideh Ala'i, and Susana Castiglione for their continuous support and assistance while The Arbitration Brief reorganized over this past calendar year. Additionally, without guidance from the Center on Commercial International Arbitration, this publication would not have been possible. Lastly, I would like to express my deepest gratitude to the brief's talented editorial board, staff, and additional contributors who worked tirelessly to make this issue a reality.

Please explore our website for more information about The Arbitration Brief. If you have any questions, please feel free to reach out to arbitrationbrief@wcl.american.edu.

Best Regards,
Adam Briscoe
Editor-in-Chief
Volume 5

THE ARBITRATION BRIEF

Volume 5

The Arbitration Brief is a student publication of American University Washington College of Law prepared with the assistance of the Washington College of Law Center on International Commercial Arbitration. The mission of this publication is to provide timely information, both practical and academic, on developments in the field of arbitration. We welcome pieces from academics, practicing attorneys, arbitrators, and students. For more information, please contact arbitrationbrief@wcl.american.edu. The views expressed in this publication are those of the writers and are not necessarily those of the editors, the Center on International Commercial Arbitration, or American University.

Table of Contents

CORRUPTION IN INTERNATIONAL COMMERCIAL ARBITRATION: ARBITRABILITY, ADMISSIBILITY & ADJUDICATION

Deeksha Malik & Geetanjali Kamat

INTRODUCTION: CORRUPTION AND ITS CONDEMNATION

In an era which is audience to the burgeoning increase in the utilization of international commercial arbitration, questions that affect the legality of the proceeding itself need to be microscopically examined. Although matters such as breach of warranty and *force majeure* are globally recognized concepts that are legally enforceable by parties, issues of corruption are yet to be conclusively and statutorily prohibited in the field of international commercial arbitration. Allegations of bribery by one party upon another have several adverse consequences; as it may not only impede the performance of the contract itself, but also may result in impairing friendly relations between countries in the international matrix of trade and commerce. Though there are neither any particular set of restrictions that have been expressly laid down with respect to such allegations nor the pronouncement of any rules that strictly condemn the same, the global aversion to such misconduct is palpable. Thus, international concern in this regard has morphed into the current *vox populi*, through the ratification of various international conventions that prohibit corruption in international commercial arbitration. As a result thereof, this only makes the case stronger to have instances of corruption prohibited in a more vociferous manner unlike the lukewarm response it has been receiving from the international actors so far.

The fundamental existence of law requires it to be in tune with the spirit of the society that it seeks to protect and must accordingly amend itself periodically. The modern trend with respect to international commercial arbitration has moved towards "zero tolerance" of corruption, which arbitrators have become compelled to address.[1] For instance, the 1977 US Foreign Corrupt Practice Act, and the 2010 UK Bribery Act incorporate obligations upon state parties that have an extra-jurisdictional reach up to a certain extent. This implies that arbitrators who act outside the domestic jurisdiction in such countries may need to take into account the criminal offenses that have been stated under such legislation. The US Foreign Corrupt Practice Act strictly prohibits anyone acting within the territorial limits of the United States from 'making or even offering to make corrupt payments to a foreign public official' in order to secure an improper advantage.[2]

In the year 1989, the Organization for Economic Cooperation and Development ("OECD") began deliberating and discussing the issue of combating illicit payments in international business

---

[1] *See* James D. Wolfensohn, *The Right Wheel: An Agenda for Comprehensive Development, in* VOICE FOR THE WORLD'S POOR: SELECTED SPEECHES AND WRITINGS OF WORLD BANK PRESIDENT JAMES D. WOLFENSOHN, 138, 140 (James D. Wolfensohn ed., 2005).

[2] CRIMINAL DIV. U.S. DEP'T JUSTICE & ENFORCEMENT DIV. U.S. SEC. & EXCH. COMM'N, A RESOURCE GUIDE TO THE U.S. FOREIGN CORRUPT PRACTICES ACT (November 2012), https://www.sec.gov/spotlight/fcpa/fcpa-resource-guide.pdf.

transactions.[3] In order to fulfill this objective, various OECD committees were assigned the task of studying multiple facets of corruption. Consequently, in 1994, the OECD adopted 'Recommendations on Bribery in International Business Transactions', which directed member countries to take effective measures to deter, prevent, and combat the bribery of foreign public officials in connection with international business transactions.[4] In 1996, the OECD Committee on International Investment and Multinational Enterprises reported to the Council of Ministers the mechanism through which member countries can be encouraged to criminalize bribery of foreign public officials.[5] However, even amidst such progress, these recommendations mainly went to the extent of advising countries to adopt measures by way of domestic legislations in order to monitor their progress on fulfillment of the OECD Recommendations. Unfortunately, while the US vehemently voiced their support for a "full-scale binding treaty" in order to have a statutorily binding force upon the countries, European countries preferred non-binding recommendations that did not have any adverse legal consequences for any failure to adhere to these recommendations.[6] Ultimately, it was in the year 1997 that the 'OECD Convention on Combating Bribery of Foreign Public Officials in International Business Transactions' came into the limelight. Although this convention declares bribery of foreign officials as illegal in its preamble, it clearly binds countries to "enact appropriate legislation", thereby keeping in line with the essence of

---

[3] *See* Mark Pieth, *International Cooperation to Combat Corruption, in* PETERSON INST. FOR INT'L ECON., CORRUPTION AND THE GLOBAL ECONOMY, 119, 122–23 (Kimberly Ann Elliott ed., 1997).

[4] *See* David A. Gantz, *Globalizing Sanctions Against Foreign Bribery: The Emergence of a New International Legal Consensus*, 18 NW. J. INT'L L. & BUS. 457, 483–84 (1997).

[5] COMM. ON INT'L INV. & MULTINATIONAL ENTERS., ORG. FOR ECON. CO-OPERATION & DEV., REVIEW OF THE 1994 RECOMMENDATION ON BRIBERY IN INTERNATIONAL BUSINESS TRANSACTIONS, INCLUDING PROPOSALS TO FACILITATE THE CRIMINALISATION OF BRIBERY OF FOREIGN PUBLIC OFFICIALS, 3 (1997), *available at* http://www.oecd.org/officialdocuments/publicdisplaydocumentpdf/?cote=OCDE /GD(97)131&docLanguage=En.

[6] *Id.* at 195.

the treaty itself.[7] The truth of the matter is that corruption involves matters of general interest to society at large. There have been several instances of arbitration proceedings that have emphasized good morals and ethics of international trade and transnational public policy.[8]

This paper seeks to examine the perplexing issues that arise within the context of international commercial arbitrations involving allegations of corruption. Part I begins with a discussion on the issue of whether it is within the capacity of an arbitrator to deal with a claim of corruption, especially when there is a trend of growing acceptance towards the recognition of corruption as a matter of public policy. Part II then delves into the various aspects that concern the adjudication of corruption by an arbitrator. Finally, Part C considers the legal consequences that follow from a finding of corruption by an arbitrator.

I. Arbitrability of Corruption in International Commercial Arbitration

The moot point in this section is whether allegations of corruption are capable of being referred to and settled by an arbitrator. Arbitrability as a concept is often at loggerheads with the parties' freedom to decide what should and should not be adjudicated by the tribunal. The matter becomes more complex when juxtaposed with concerns of public policy. This is the case with corruption, as we shall see.

A. Party Autonomy Vis-A-Vis Arbitrability

One of the significant principles that arbitration espouses is that of party autonomy, which essentially connotes the freedom of the parties to decide how their disputes are to be resolved. Both national laws and international arbitral institutions and organizations endorse

---

[7] *See id.* at 215.
[8] *See id.* at 213.

this principle without any significant opposition.[9] This doctrine is often confronted by the notion of arbitrability, or more specifically 'objective arbitrability,' which raises the question as to whether a particular type of issue is amenable to resolution by arbitration.[10]

Each State determines the categories of cases which are to be kept out of the jurisdiction of an arbitral tribunal in accordance with its own political, social, and economic policies.[11] Some commentators hold the view that there is no internationally accepted opinion as to what matters are arbitrable, as each country has its own perspectives on legality and illegality.[12] For instance, within the EU, "disputes directly affecting the existence or validity of a registered intellectual property right are considered non-arbitrable."[13] This is so despite the fact that intellectual property rights are regarded as freely disposable by the owner. The rationale behind this rule is difficult to be laid down in exact terms; some suggest that the State would naturally want to exercise control over the granting of IP rights, as these constitute national assets and contribute significantly to economic growth.[14] Some countries, such as Brazil, accord different treatment to infringement and validity issues.[15] Therefore, while issues such as patent licensing, franchising agreements, trademark assignments and the like are capable of settlement by arbitration, disputes relating to validity raise public order issues, which render them inarbitrable.[16] Similar concerns have been raised in respect to disputes involving competition and anti-trust questions.

---

[9] *See* ALAN REDFERN & MARTIN HUNTER, LAW AND PRACTICE OF INTERNATIONAL COMMERCIAL ARBITRATION 315 (4th ed. 2004).

[10] *See* Ilias Bantekas, *The Foundations of Arbitrability in International Commercial Arbitration,* 27 AUSTRALIAN Y.B. Int'l L. 193, 193 (2008).

[11] *See* NIGEL BLACKABY, CONSTANTINE PARTASIDES, ALAN REDFERN & MARTIN HUNTER, REDFERN AND HUNTER ON INTERNATIONAL ARBITRATION 124 (5th ed. 2009).

[12] *See* ANDREW TWEEDDALE & KEREN TWEEDDALE, ARBITRATION OF COMMERCIAL DISPUTES: INTERNATIONAL AND ENGLISH LAW AND PRACTICE §4.23 (2007).

[13] JULIAN D.M. LEW, LOUKAS A. MISTELIS & STEFAN KRÖLL, COMPARATIVE INTERNATIONAL COMMERCIAL ARBITRATION 209 (2003).

[14] *See* Bantekas, *supra* note 10, at 213.

[15] William Grantham, *The Arbitrability of International Intellectual Property Disputes,* 14 BERKELEY J. INT'L. L. 173, 216–217 (1996).

[16] *Id.*

Before 1985, for example, the position in the United States was that "the pervasive public interest in the enforcement of the anti-trust laws and the nature of the claims that arise in such case, combine to make anti-trust claims inappropriate for arbitration."[17] The position somewhat changed after the US Supreme Court decision in the case of *Mitsubishi Motors Corp v. Soler Chrysler-Plymouth Inc.,*[18] wherein the Court purported to establish a pro-arbitration atmosphere by holding that the mere existence of an anti-trust issue does not *per se* lead to invalidation of the selected forum.[19] The Court opined:

> "...concerns of international comity, respect for the capacities of foreign and transnational tribunals, and sensitivity to the need of the international commercial system for predictability in the resolution of disputes require that we enforce the parties' agreement, even assuming that a contrary result would be forthcoming in a domestic context."[20]

In conclusion, the differences among national legal systems in respect to some issues of arbitrability can be contrasted to arbitral disputes involving allegations of bribery (or corruption), as this is an issue that perturbs almost every jurisdiction.

B. Arbitrability & Public Policy

Public policy is one term that is notoriously difficult to define. In 1853, the House of Lords observed that public policy is "that principle of law which holds that no subject can lawfully do that which has a tendency to be injurious to the public or public good."[21] Others have variously defined the term as the forum state's most

---

[17] Am. Safety Equip. Corp. v. J.P. Maguire & Co., 391 F.2d 821, 827–28 (2d Cir. 1968).

[18] 473 U.S. 614, 629 (1985).

[19] *Id.* at 615.

[20] *Id.* at 629 (noting that the reasoning adopted by the Supreme Court compels one to question whether the decision would have been the same had the facts of the case been purely in the domestic context).

[21] Egerton v. Lord Brownlow, [1853] 4 H.L. 1, 196.

basic notions of morality and justice,[22] or a rule which reflects the fundamental economic, legal, moral, political, religious, and social standards of every State or extra-national community,[23] something which must be upheld without exception.

The discourse on public policy brings to light the distinction between international and transnational public policy. International public policy (which is considered to be narrower than domestic public policy) is State-specific, meaning that its content and application depends on the State where it is being used. For example, it has been noted in respect of the French legislation that "the international public policy to which Article 1502.5 refers can only mean the French conception of international public policy or, in other words, the set of values a breach of which could not be tolerated by the French legal order, even in international cases."[24] Transnational public policy, on the other hand, relates to rules which are universally recognized as being most basic. In other words, it comprises "fundamental rules of natural law, principles of universal justice, *jus cogens* in public international law, and the general principles of morality accepted by what are referred to as civili[z]ed nations." The scope of this concept is certainly narrower than that of international public policy, for very few norms are of such nature that their breach would shock the conscience of most, if not all, the civilized nations. The difficulty in identifying such norms is one crucial factor which leads courts and arbitral tribunals to apply the concept of international public policy as conceived by a particular State, which is, more often than not, the seat of the arbitral tribunal (*lex loci arbitri*) in matters of arbitrability.[25]

Arbitrability and public policy have a close connection. The relation is founded on the premise that public policy refers to imperative rules of a State or transnational community and the issues related thereto have a significant bearing on the public at large. The

---

[22] *See* Parsons & Whittemore Overseas Co. v. Societe Generale de L'Industrie du Papier, 508 F.2d 969, 974 (2d. Cir. 1974).

[23] *See* LEW, MISTELIS & KROLL, *supra* note 13, at 422.

[24] FOUCHARD GALLARD GOLDMAN ON INTERNATIONAL COMMERCIAL ARBITRATION §1648 (Emmanuel Gaillard & John Savage eds., 1999).

[25] Loukas A. Mistelis, *Is Arbitrability a National or an International Law Issue?*, *in* ARBITRABILITY: INTERNATIONL AND COMPARATIVE PERSPECTIVES 1, 13 (Loukas A. Mistelis & Stavros L. Brekoulakis eds., 2009).

element of public interest makes such issues incapable of reference to a private settlement process.[26]

The case of *Silica Investors Ltd. v. Tomolugen Holdings Ltd.*,[27] decided by the High Court of Singapore, is particularly relevant at this juncture. Parties entered into a share sale agreement which, *inter alia,* had an arbitration clause. The plaintiff brought a minority oppression claim against the defendants, seeking relief in the nature of a buyout order and an order for winding up of the company. The defendants applied for a stay of the proceedings, which was denied by the court, and the defendants proceeded to appeal. One of the issues at hand was whether the plaintiff's claim was arbitrable. The High Court found that the claim certainly fell within the scope of the terms of the arbitration clause, namely, "arising out of or in connection with this Agreement." However, this should not mean that the matter was necessarily arbitrable.

The Court analyzed the position of law in England (where a minority oppression claim is arbitrable, though the scope of the relief sought would be limited in cases where the interests of the other shareholders would be affected), Australia (where the said claim is arbitrable in so far as the remedies sought are *inter partes* and not *in rem*), and Canada (where the issue is unsettled). Thereafter, it observed with respect to the law in Singapore that no general conclusion could be reached. However-

> "...many if not most of the minority oppression claims under s. 216 of the CA [Companies Act], claims will be non-arbitrable. This will often be in cases where, e.g., there are other shareholders who are not parties to the arbitration, or the arbitral award will directly affect third parties or the general public, or some claims fall within the scope of the arbitration clause and some do not, or there are overtones of insolvency, or the remedy or relief that is sought is one that an arbitral tribunal is unable to make."[28]

---

[26] *See* James D. Fry, *Désordre Public International Under the New York Convention: Wither Truly International Public Policy,* CHINESE J. INT'L L., 81, 85 (2009).

[27] *See generally* Silica Investors Ltd. v. Tomolugen Holdings Ltd., [2014]SGHC 101 (Sing.).

[28] Companies Act 2006, §142 (Eng.).

The above illustration shows that courts would refuse to uphold arbitrability in a matter that has ramifications on the interests of the parties, such that the dispute would no longer remain a private one.

There may, however, be situations where arbitrability and public policy do not overlap, as can be understood from the instances mentioned in the previous section. Thus, disputes relating to intellectual property rights might be regarded by a State to be within exclusive judicial jurisdiction, though such disputes may not have any impact whatsoever on the public interest. This distinction can be clearly seen in the New York Convention.[29] Article V lists out the grounds upon which the recognition and enforcement of an arbitral award may be refused. The second part of this Article provides for two grounds which, if found by the Court upon an application of a party or otherwise, the award could be set aside. These are (a) the subject-matter of the dispute in question is non-arbitrable, or (b) the recognition or enforcement of the award is contrary to public policy.[30] Therefore, laws restricting arbitrability may not form part of the mandatory rules of public policy.

The following section discusses how the public policy exception to arbitrability is applied to cases pertaining to corruption.

C. Corruption And The Exception of Public Policy to Arbitrability

Anyone engaged in cross-border or international commercial transactions would acknowledge that corruption and bribery are worldwide problems that plague good governance and seriously impede performance of commercial agreements.[31] An estimate by the World Economic Forum shows that the cost of corruption comes to more than 5% of the global GDP (around US$ 2.6 trillion), thereby escalating the cost of doing business by nearly 10%

---

[29] *See generally* Convention on the Recognition and Enforcement of Foreign Arbitral Awards, June 10, 1958, 21 U.S.T. 2517, 330 U.N.T.S. 38 [hereinafter New York Convention].

[30] *See id.* art. V(2).

[31] William Fox, *Adjudicating Bribery and Corruption Issues in International Commercial Arbitration,* 27 J. ENERGY & NAT. RESOURCES L. 487, 487 (2009).

globally.[32] In the public sector, funds contributed by the people end up in private pockets and thereby adversely affecting growth, infrastructure, and public services. It is precisely because of these reasons why corruption is forbidden by a number of international conventions, especially the United Nations Convention against Corruption[33] and the OECD Convention on Combating Bribery of Foreign Public Officials in International Business Transactions.[34]

Arbitration law has witnessed a head on collision between corruption and public policy. One instance is the famous 1963 ICC Award[35] authored by Judge Lagergren. The case concerned a public works contract, wherein an Argentinean agent was supposed to receive a "commission" from the Respondent (a company that was competing for a certain contract), in return for his exertion of influence on Argentinean government officials at that point in time. The company refused to pay, thereby triggering a dispute between the parties. The learned Judge observed that although the relevant documents bore semblance to an ordinary legal commercial agreement, the evidence revealed that a substantial part of the commission was to be used for bribes. Accordingly, the arbitrator had no jurisdiction with respect to the matter, as contracts which seriously violate *bonos mores* or international public policy are unenforceable to say the least, and as such, cannot be sanctioned by courts or arbitrators. Therefore, it was held:

> "Whether one is taking the point of view of good government or that of commercial ethics it is impossible to close one's eyes to the probable destination of amounts of this magnitude, and to the destructive effect thereof on the

---

[32] Global Agenda Council, *Anti-Corruption*, WORLD ECONOMIC FORUM, http://reports.weforum.org/global-agenda-council-2012/councils/anti-corruption/, (2012–2013).

[33] G. A. Res. 58/4, United Nations Convention Against Corruption, (Oct. 31, 2003). (As of July 2010, there are 146 parties to this Convention).

[34] ORGANISATION FOR ECONOMIC CO-OPERATION AND DEVELOPMENT. WORKING GROUP ON BRIBERY IN INTERNATIONAL BUSINESS TRANSACTIONS, CONVENTION ON COMBATING BRIBERY OF FOREIGN PUBLIC OFFICIALS IN INTERNATIONAL BUSINESS TRANSACTIONS : AND RELATED DOCUMENTS (OECD) (1998).

[35] *See generally* Case No. 1110 of 1963, 10 Arb. Int'l 282 (ICC Int'l Ct. Arb,).

business pattern with consequent impairment of industrial progress. Such corruption is an international evil; it is contrary to good morals and to an international public policy common to the community of nations."[36]

This principle was reiterated in the *World Duty Free* case,[37] wherein the Tribunal noted that bribery is contrary to the international public policy of most, if not all, States.

Over the years, however, owing to the doctrine of separability, there has been general acceptance, both nationally and internationally, that an allegation of bribery does not itself deprive the arbitrator of jurisdiction over the dispute.[38] In one case, it was noted that even though the arbitrators were well aware of the allegations that commitments made by public-sector entities in respect to certain major projects were devoid of economic contribution to public welfare, such allegations are required to be proven, which in this case, was not done.[39] Recent case law is in tune with this precedent, allowing an arbitrator to rule on illegality for bribery. Once bribery is proven, the tribunal declares the contract unenforceable. One author has stated:

"If an allegation of corruption is made in plain language in the course of arbitration proceedings, the arbitral tribunal is clearly under a duty to consider the allegation and to decide whether or not it is proved...A failure to address the existence of such illegality may threaten the enforceability of the award, and thus may sit uncomfortably with an arbitral tribunal's duty to under some modern rules of arbitration to use its best endeavors to ensure that it's award is enforceable."[40]

---

[36] *Id.* at 20.

[37] World Duty Free Company Ltd. v. The Republic of Kenya, ICSID Case No. ARB/00/7, Award (October 4, 2006).

[38] *See* ALAN REDFERN, MARTIN HUNTER, NIGEL BLACKABY & CONSTANTINE PARTASIDES, LAW AND PRACTICE OF INTERNATIONAL COMMERCIAL ARBITRATION 143 (2004).

[39] Final Award of 4 May 1999, Himpurna California Energy Ltd. v. Perusahaan Listruik Negara, 25 ICCA Y.B. Comm.l Arb., 13, 44 (ICC Int'l Ct. Arb.).

[40] REDFERN, HUNTER, BLACKABY & PARTASIDES, *supra* note 38, at 144.

The rationale behind this approach is simple: when parties choose to refer their disputes to an arbitral tribunal, they cannot be presumed to intend that the issue of validity be decided by a court. The House of Lords held in *Fiona* that "very clear language" would need to be found before deciding that the parties had such an intention.[41] "If arbitrators can decide whether a contract is void for initial illegality, there is no reason why they should not decide whether a contract has been procured by bribery, just as much as they can decide whether a contract has been procured by misrepresentation or non-disclosure."[42]

Many contemporary thinkers are of the view that arbitration is a normal forum, if not the *juge naturel*, as far as cross-border transactions are concerned.[43] In such a scenario, it is inappropriate to hold that arbitrators are incapable of dealing with issues where public interest or protection of weaker parties[44] is involved, or that arbitrators are insensitive to considerations of equity.[45]

II. Adjudicating Bribery in International Commercial Arbitration

On an international level, the mere allegation of corruption made by one party against the other bears immense gravity as it is likely to have an adverse effect on the reputation of a State party. This nuanced situation becomes more pronounced when understood within the context of international commercial arbitration.

When it comes to scrutinizing evidence with respect to issues of corruption in the field of international commercial arbitration, three points of consideration need to be taken into account. First, there exists the possibility of an adverse effect on the rule of burden of proof. Second, indirect evidence needs to be

---

[41] *See* Fiona Trust Holding Corp v. Privalov, [2007] 4 All ER 951 (HL) (Eng.).

[42] *Id.*

[43] *See* Yves Derains, *Chroniques de Sentences Arbitrales*, 105 JOURNAL DU DROIT INTERNATIONAL (CLUNET), 976 (1978).

[44] *See* Fulham Football Club (1987) Ltd v. Richards, [2011] EWCA (Civ) 855, [333] (Eng.) (stating that in England, for instance, issues pertaining to rights of minority shareholders can be dealt with by an arbitrator).

[45] *See* Pierre Mayer, *La règle morale dans l'arbitrage international*, *in* PIERRE BELLET, ETUDES OFFERTES À PIERRE BELLET (1991).

critically evaluated and thereafter, permitted to be brought before the tribunal. Third, there is an urgent need to strengthen the standard of proof in cases of serious allegations, especially where concerns of public policy, fraud, or corruption are at issue.

Thus, it is not without reason that there has been considerable debate on the issue of evidence brought forth by parties before the tribunal. In circumstances when there is a *prima facie* suggestion of corruption and neither party brings forth any allegations of such wrongdoing, the question remains whether tribunals are legally empowered to inquire into issues of corruption *sua sponte*. Moreover, the requisite standard of proof that needs to be discharged, in order to successfully prove a case of corruption, needs to be conclusively determined, as the integrity and fairness of the arbitral process are regarded as paramount.

With this background, this article will now examine the various evidentiary issues pertaining to both international commercial arbitration, and arbitration in general.

A. Evidence-Taking Mechanisms in Arbitration

The procedure for submitting and disclosing evidentiary materials plays an essential role in international commercial arbitration, as "fact-finding" is one of the primary functions of arbitral tribunals. While courts in most civil law jurisdictions do not provide for party-initiated disclosure of evidence, common law jurisdictions derive their genesis from the adversarial system of justice and strictly adhere to the party-initiated disclosure process.[46]

At the international level, certain rules have been developed to address the evidence-taking mechanism irrespective of the legal system. Article 20 of the ICC arbitration rules provides that the tribunal shall proceed within as short a time as possible in order to establish the facts of the case by "all appropriate means."[47] The term "all appropriate means" implies that the tribunal is endowed with

---

[46] Claudia T. Salomon & Sandra Friedrich, *Obtaining and Submitting Evidence in International Arbitration in the United States*, 24 Am. Rev. Int'l Arb. 549, 550 (2013).

[47] The Chamber of Arbitration of Milan Rules: A Commentary 546 (Ugo Draetta & Riccardo Luzzatto eds., 2012).

flexibility in taking evidence from concerned parties. However, even the slightest possibility of misinterpreting such ambiguity can adversely impact the judicious nature of arbitration proceedings itself. Meanwhile, the UNCITRAL Arbitration Rules provide that at any time during the arbitral proceedings, the tribunal may require the parties to produce documents, exhibits or other evidence within a definite period of time that shall be determined at the discretion of the tribunal.[48]

The International Bar Association has also placed an emphasis upon the quality of evidence that ought to be presented by the parties and has implemented Rules on the Taking of Evidence in International Commercial Arbitration which, *inter alia*, state that every Party is entitled to know, reasonably in advance, of the evidence upon which the other Parties rely.[49] This permits the other Party to prepare his defense and expedites the entire proceeding in a fair and transparent manner. While Article 3 of the IBA Rules provides for the discovery and production of documents, Article 4 permits a party to obtain the testimony of voluntary witnesses or persons who will not appear voluntarily.

Though these rules are not precise in a 'mandatory' sense for any particular international arbitration institution to follow, it is ultimately up to the will of the parties to incorporate the rules in the arbitration clause that governs their commercial relationship.

B. Rules Governing Adjudication of Bribery

Though the "choice of law" provision is still made available to the parties, the risk associated with such liberty is that it gives them the autonomy to choose a law that may not be as stringent with certain forms of bribery in international commercial arbitration as it ought to be. As a form of practice, the arbitral tribunal does observe the mandatory rules of the country where the contract between the two parties is performed. However, those rules that specifically seek to protect legitimate goals will be placed on a higher pedestal than

---

[48] CHRISTOPHER DUGAN DON WALLACE, NOAH RUBINS & BORZU SABAHI, INVESTOR-STATE ARBITRATION 161 (2011).

[49] Anna Magdalena Kubalczyk, *Evidentiary Rules in International Arbitration: A Comparative Analysis of Approaches and the Need for Regulation*, 3 GRONINGEN J. INT'L L. 85, 107 (2015).

other rules. For instance, a provision of *lex loci solutionis*, which seeks to impose an indiscriminate ban upon intermediaries, is less likely to be enforced in the field of international commercial arbitration than an internationally condemned act such as private bribery. This proposition follows from the fact that as a matter of practice and principle, transnational beliefs that find support from a majority of countries ought to be given much more importance than domestic beliefs in order to accommodate an 'international' stance within the system of commercial arbitration itself. Another aspect that is worthy of attention is the fact that there needs to be a sufficient nexus between *lex arbitri* and the case itself; this implies that the concerned case must *expressly* affect public interest in a *manifest manner*.[50]

C. Burden and Standard of Proof

Commentators belonging to various jurisdictions have different views as to which law should be applied to determine the standard of proof related to proving corruption. While some argue that the substantive law chosen by the parties should govern the same,[51] others suggest that the applicable procedural rules are more appropriate.[52] There are, however, various rules that have a general application irrespective of the governing law. Evaluation of evidence is done on the basis of these rules as per the discretion of the arbitrator.

Very few rules deal with the issue of burden and standard of proof in international arbitration. One of them is the 2013 UNCITRAL Arbitration Rules, wherein it is provided that each party shall have the burden of proving the facts relied upon to support its claim or defense.[53] However, a vexing factor in proving

---

[50] Vladimir Pavic, *Bribery and International Commercial Arbitration: The Role of Mandatory Rules and Public Policy*, 43 VICTORIA U. WELLINGTON L. REV. 661, 676 (2012).

[51] KLAUS PETER BERGER, INTERNATIONAL ECONOMIC ARBITRATION 444–50 (1993).

[52] Haugeneder & Liebscher, *Chapter V: Investment Arbitration: Corruption and Investment Arbitration: Substantive Standards and Proof, in* AUSTRIAN ARBITRATION YEARBOOK 2009 539, 545 (Christian Klausegger, et al. eds., 2009).

[53] G.A. Res. 68/109, art. 27 (December 16, 2013).

corruption is that, like most crimes and cases of grave or fraudulent misconduct, corruption is specifically designed not to be detected.[54] Various arbitral tribunals have expressed the view that it is "notoriously difficult" to prove corruption, for there is little or no physical evidence in relation thereto.[55] In such a situation, placing the burden of proof on the party alleging so might be too onerous. At the same time, the rule that a party must prove the facts upon which it bases its claim is regarded as a rule of natural justice and due process.[56] Indeed, the existence of this principle is necessary to negate the possibility of parties making groundless allegations against each other, particularly when the party seeks to prove a startling proposition, such as corruption.[57]

The problem with corruption is that even if the circumstances are suspicious, it is difficult to meet a high standard of proof. In a majority of cases, it has been propounded that the usual standard of "preponderance of probabilities" is sufficient in circumstances of corruption.[58] On the other hand, the principle of "clear and convincing evidence" has been proposed in adjudication of corruption, as demonstrated in the case of *Dadras v. Iran*, where the arbitral tribunal opined that the applicability of this principle finds support in both American and English law, according to which cases of fraudulent behavior mandate a higher standard of proof.[59] In similar terms, the arbitral tribunal in the famous *Westinghouse* case noted that matters like fraud must be proven to exist by clear and

---

[54] Karen Mills, *Corruption and Other Illegality in the Formation and Performance of Contracts and in the Conduct of Arbitrations Relating Thereto*, in 11 ICCA CONGRESS SERIES 288, 295 (2003).
[55] EDF (Services) Ltd. v. Romania, ICSID Case No. ARB/05/13, Award, 64 §221 (8 October 2009).
[56] *Summary of the Chatham House International Law Discussion Group Meeting on 28 March 2007*, CHATHAM HOUSE (Mar. 28, 2007), https://www.chathamhouse.org/sites/default/files/public/Research/International%20Law/il280307.pdf.
[57] J. Martin Hunter, *Modern Trends in the Presentation of Evidence in International Commercial Arbitration*, 3 AM. REV. INT'L ARB. 204, 211 (1992).
[58] Constantine Partasides, *Proving Corruption in International Arbitration: A Balanced Standard for the Real World*, 25 ICSID Rev. Foreign Investment L.J. 47, §22 (2010).
[59] Dadras International v. Islamic Republic of Iran, Case Nos. 213 & 215,31 Iran-USCTR 127, 135—36, Award (1995).

convincing evidence, and cannot be justified by mere speculation because of the seriousness of the allegations.[60] The bar was raised in the *Hilmarton* case, where the tribunal reasoned that it was necessary for the party to prove bribery beyond doubt, although it could be done by indirect evidence.[61] One might argue that such standard of proof is required only in criminal cases because they entail penal consequences, something which an arbitrator cannot sanction, and therefore, applying such a standard in arbitration is unwarranted. Constantine Partasides has argued that arbitral tribunals should ordinarily adopt a balanced approach, neither relaxing the standard of proof nor making it severe for a party to discharge the burden.[62]

A significant aspect in this discourse is the circumstance of the case. If the arbitrator notices, on the basis of the facts presented before them, that there are some "red flags" pointing towards to the existence of corruption, it may call upon the other party to explain them, and on its failure to do so, draw an adverse inference against the other party.[63] The Resource Guide to the 1977 US Foreign Corrupt Practices Act has provided illustrations of "red flags," some of them being unusual payment patterns, history of corruption in the country, lack of transparency in books of accounts, lack of qualifications on the part of the service-provider, and so on.[64]

Such a situation took place in the case of *Metal-Tech Ltd. v. Republic of Uzbekistan*.[65] The facts of the case brought to light

---

[60] Westinghouse and Burns & Roe v. National Power Company, Case No. 621 of ,1991, 7 Mealey's Int'l. Arb. Rep., 31 (ICC Int'l Ct. Arb.).

[61] ICC Case No. 5622 of 1988, *in* 19 Y.B, Comm. Arb., 105, 111 (ICC Int'l Ct. Arb.).

[62] Kyriaki Karadelis, *Corruption and the Standard of Proof*, Global Arbitration Review (July 26, 2010), http://globalarbitrationreview.com/article/1029476/corruption-and-the-standard-of-proof.

[63] Even the International Bar Association [IBA] Rules on the Taking of Evidence in International Arbitration provide that an arbitral tribunal may draw adverse inferences if a party fails, without satisfactory explanation, to make available relevant evidence.

[64] CRIMINAL DIV. U.S. DEP'T JUSTICE & ENFORCEMENT DIV. U.S. SEC. & EXCH. COMM'N, *supra* note 2.

[65] Metal-Tech Ltd v. Republic of Uzbekistan, ICSID Case No. ARB/10/03, Award (October 4, 2013).

certain "red flags" such as lack of requisite qualifications of the consultants, exorbitant "remuneration" paid to such consultants, and close relations with high level government officials, including the President and the Prime Minister of Uzbekistan. Moreover, the party against whom corruption was alleged did not offer any explanation on how exactly the consultants provided support to Metal-Tech's investment.[66] Accordingly, the tribunal held that though there was no direct proof, the unexplained circumstances were such that they led to the conclusion that bribery had actually been committed.[67]

In light of the foregoing discussion, the authors submit that the burden of proof must lie with the person alleging that the contract in question is tainted with bribery, as is the case with other forms of illegality. The authors also believe that there must certainly be a higher standard of proof than a mere preponderance of probabilities in regards to a sensitive issue like corruption. However, such standard should not be as high as "beyond doubt" for the simple reason that this would allow the wrongdoers to escape the clutches of the law, considering the paucity of evidence that exists in such cases. It must, therefore, lie somewhere between the two.[68]

D. Sua Sponte Investigation of Bribery by Arbitration

Another issue that has been in controversy is whether an arbitrator can initiate, *sua sponte*, an investigation of bribery. It is not always the case that one of the parties comes forward with a specific allegation of corruption against the other. There could be a situation where suspicious circumstances come to the attention of the arbitral tribunal as the arbitration proceedings progress. Thus, the question to be addressed at this juncture is whether it is possible for an arbitral tribunal to investigate possible bribery on its own accord, without there being any such specific allegation from either party? On the one hand, it is argued that the essence of arbitration is the will of the parties to refer specific issues to such private adjudication, and therefore, an arbitrator cannot stray into an *ultra*

---

[66] *Id.* at §217.
[67] *Id.* at §243.
[68] Waguih Elie George Siag & Clorinda Vecchi v. Arab Republic of Egypt, ICSID Case No. ARB/05/15, Award (June 1, 2009).

petita area[69] and impose his own will onto proceedings by inquiring into a matter not brought before the tribunal. If the arbitrator does so, the award passed by him may be set aside[70] or refused recognition and enforcement[71] on the grounds that the tribunal exceeded its authority.

On the other hand, if arbitral awards are as binding as a decision rendered by a court,[72] it is imperative that the arbitral tribunal treats such matters in the same manner as a court, and its failure to do so would be tantamount to endorsing bribery.[73] The argument that an arbitrator would exceed his mandate by ruling upon the existence and consequences of corruption is also challenged by some who contend that a suspected or manifest illegality, which is relevant to the claims or defenses cannot be isolated. It was observed by the Singapore Court of Appeal in the case of *CRW Joint Operation v. PT Perusahaan Gas Negara (Persero) TBK* that in determining whether an arbitrator has exceeded his authority in considering and deciding a particular matter, its relevance to the issues submitted by the parties to the tribunal for resolution is a crucial factor to be considered.[74]

The authors agree with the latter approach. Even though arbitration is a creature of contract, an arbitral tribunal cannot ignore international condemnation of bribery. It is difficult to ignore the tribunal's comment in *Himpurna California Energy Ltd. v. PLN,*

---

[69] BLACKABY, PARTASIDES, REDFERN & HUNTER, *supra* note 11, §2.140.

[70] Report of UNCITRAL on the Work of its Eighteenth Session, U.N. Doc. A/40/17 (1985) (as amended in 2006), art. 34(2)(a)(iii) [hereinafter UNCITRAL Model Law]("34[...] (2) An arbitral award may be set aside by the court specified in article 6 only if: (a) the party making the application furnishes proof that: [...] (iii) the award deals with a dispute not contemplated by or not falling within the terms of the submission to arbitration, or contains decisions on matters beyond the scope of the submission to arbitration.").

[71] Article 36(1)(a)(iii) of the UNCITRAL Model Law and Article V(1)(c) of the New York Convention provide for refusal of enforcement of an award on the same basis as setting aside an award under Article 34(2)(a)(iii) of the UNCITRAL Model Law. *See id.* art. 36(1)(a)(iii); New York Convention *supra* note 29, art. V(1)(c).

[72] UNCITRAL Model Law, *supra* note 70, art. 35(1).

[73] Nick Neocleous, *Arbitrators' Investigative Rights and Duties*, Kiev Arbitration Days (2014), *available at* http://uba.ua/documents/doc/nick_neocleous.pdf, at 14.

[74] [2011] SGCA 33 (Sing.).

that the members of an arbitral tribunal do not live in an ivory tower, and that the arbitral process cannot be divorced from reality.[75] A tribunal must remain vigilant and check for the possibility of corrupt dealings by one or both parties to arbitration. Any failure or laxity in this regard may open the arbitral award to annulment or non-recognition,[76] or may hold the arbitrator liable for failure to act.[77] Therefore, it should be within an arbitrator's mandate to make investigation *sua sponte* if he or she is of the opinion that some corrupt activities are afoot, provided such activities have nexus with the matters which have been referred to arbitration.

III. Consequences of a Finding of Corruption

The dilemma of an arbitrator does not end at the issues of arbitrability and standard of proof required in the case of corruption. Once a finding of corruption has been reached, either upon the evidence led by the alleging party or upon a *sua sponte* investigation, the arbitrator also has to decide the consequences of such finding on the contract itself, and ultimately, on the respective claims of the parties.

Most domestic legal systems recognize a distinction between contracts aimed at corruption (either expressly or impliedly) and ones procured by corruption. In the former case, there is unanimity among various jurisdictions that the contract must be declared null and void.[78] Such a consequence is not only contemplated by national

---

[75] REDFERN, HUNTER, BLACKABY & PARTASIDES, *supra* note 38, at 43.

[76] Under Articles 34(2)(b)(ii) and 36 of the UNCITRAL Model Law and Article V(2)(b) of the New York Convention, an award may be set aside or refused enforcement on public policy grounds. UNCITRAL Model Law, *supra* note 70, art. 34(2)(b)(ii), 36; New York Convention *supra* note 29, art. V(2)(b).

[77] Douglas Thomson, *Arbitrators and Corruption: Watchdogs or Bloodhounds?*, GLOB. ARBITRATION REV. (May 7, 2014), http://globalarbitrationreview.com/article/1033374/arbitrators-and-corruption-watchdogs-or-bloodhounds.

[78] *See* OBLIGATIONRECHT [OR] [THE CODE OF OBLIGATIONS] (Switz.) Art. 20, *translation at* https://www.admin.ch/opc/en/classified-compilation/19110009/201704010000/220.pdf; *see also* BÜRGERLICHES GESETZBUCH [BGB] [CIVIL CODE] § 134, *translation at* https://www.gesetze-im-internet.de/englisch_bgb/englisch_bgb.html (Ger.); *see generally* COUNCIL OF EUROPE, EXPLANATORY REPORT TO THE CIVIL LAW CONVENTION ON

laws and international conventions, but it is also regarded as a matter of transnational policy.[79] On the other hand, a contract procured by corruption remains valid until the aggrieved party takes steps towards its annulment.[80] In *World Duty Free v. Kenya*, the investor invoked ICSID arbitration wherein they admitted to have paid $2 million as a "donation" to the President of Kenya in order to do business with the Kenyan Government.[81] The arbitrator, relying on English law, which was the governing law of the contract, held that the contract was voidable at the option of Kenya, as it was procured through corruption of its agent.

It is submitted that since a contract providing for corruption is completely ineffectual, neither party can claim any remedy, contractual or restitutionary, in respect of the same. This proposition is backed by the doctrine of clean hands, or *ex turpi causa non oritur actio*, and therefore, "claims tainted by wrongdoing will not succeed, and the loss lies where it falls."[82] The idea is simple: a person cannot expect the court to come to his rescue when his own conduct is bereft of good faith and righteousness. But what would be the fate of the claims where the contract is procured by corruption? One option could be that such contract must suffer from the same consequences, for the idea is not to protect the parties but to secure public interest in detection and prevention of corruption in all its forms. The authors consider this to be too harsh for the innocent party. After rescission of the contract, the innocent party may claim *restitutio in integrum*, so that it is restored to the position it would have occupied if the contract had not been performed.[83] The

---

CORRUPTION ¶ 63 (1999) ("[I]n most European countries, the contract the cause of which is illegal is null and void.").

[79] *See* Center of Transnational Law, No. IV.7.2(a) Invalidity of Contract Due to Bribery, https://www.trans-lex.org/938000 (noting that contracts based on or involving the payment or transfer of bribes ("corruption money," "secret commissions," "pots-de-vin," "kickbacks") are void).

[80] St. John Shipping Corp. v. Joseph Rank Ltd., [1957] 1 QB 267, 283 (Eng.); *see also* Genovese v. York Lambton Corp., [1969], 1 OR 427 (Can.).

[81] ICSID Case No. ARB/00/7, *supra* note 37, at ¶ 66.

[82] Richard Kreindler, *Corruption in International Investment Arbitration: Jurisdiction and the Unclean Hands Doctrine, in* BETWEEN EAST AND WEST: ESSAYS IN HONOUR OF ULF FRANKE 309, 319 (Kaj Hobér, Annette Magnusson & Marie Öhrström eds., 2010).

[83] ICSID Case No. ARB/00/7, *supra* note 37, at ¶ 164.

2010 UNIDROIT Principles of International Commercial Contracts also lend support to this view.[84] However, care should be taken that such party is not left overcompensated, for it would mean taking advantage of the illegality of the contract.

CONCLUSION

The foregoing discussion brought to light that the issue of corruption is marred by complexity as it raises tensions between public policy matters in respect to which it is difficult to strike a balance. The authors proposed that even though corruption is subject to significant condemnation and abhorrence, it should be within an arbitrator's authority to adjudicate upon such allegations. Indeed, cross-border business transactions would suffer a setback if such issues are kept out of the scope of arbitration. We also examined the problems that arise with respect to both burden of proof and standard of proof, as it is difficult to uncover and establish corruption because of the systematic manner in which it is carried out in most cases. An attempt was made to show that it is within the power of an arbitrator to initiate a *sua sponte* investigation to unravel corruption when circumstances so warrant, for an arbitrator cannot be expected to remain a silent spectator to unscrupulous dealings. Further, we explored the consequences that a finding of corruption would bring, by making a distinction between contracts aimed at corruption and ones obtained by corruption, and arguing that in the latter case, since one of the parties is innocent, restitution may be granted if it is reasonable under the circumstances.

---

[84] INTERNATIONAL INSTITUTE FOR THE UNIFICATION OF PRIVATE LAW (UNIDROIT), PRINCIPLES OF INTERNATIONAL COMMERCIAL CONTRACTS (3d ed., 2010). Article 3.3.2(1) of the PIIC provides: "Where there has been performance under a contract infringing a mandatory rule under Article 3.3.1, restitution may be granted where this would be reasonable in the circumstances."

CAN THE LANGUAGE OF THE TRANS-PACIFIC PARTNERSHIP STILL CONTRIBUTE TO THE INTERNATIONAL INVESTMENT SYSTEM? AN ANALYSIS OF TPP'S LANGUAGE REGARDING STATES' POWERS TO REGULATE

Yurica Ramos Montes[1]

ABSTRACT

States around the world have signed several modern investment treaties and free trade agreements over the past few decades. Some of them are still in the process of being ratified, such as the Trans-Pacific Partnership (TPP). People worldwide have severely criticized the content of the TPP and have pointed out that the TPP principally protects the rights of the investors while leaving citizens

---

[1] Fellow Research Center on International Commercial Arbitration at American University Washington College of Law. Email: yuricarm@gmail.com. The opinions expressed herein are those of the author and do not represent the views of the Center. The author would also like to thank Horacio Grigera Naón and Aristeo López Sánchez for reading this article and sharing their comments with the author.

in vulnerable conditions. For instance, the language of the TPP states in general that a measure adopted by a State to protect a legitimate welfare objective should not be considered as indirect expropriation *except* in rare circumstances. This exception and other issues, regarding the regulatory powers of a State, have been at the center of several debates. This article reviews some of these debates and highlights the impact of the TPP's language for future treaties and agreements.

RESUMEN

Estados alrededor del mundo han firmado de manera creciente varios tratados modernos de inversión y acuerdos de libre comercio en las últimas décadas. Algunos de ellos todavía están en proceso de ratificación, como el Acuerdo Transpacífico de Cooperación Económica (TPP en sus siglas en ingles). Personas de todo el mundo han criticado severamente las negociaciones del TPP y han señalado que el TPP protege principalmente los derechos de los inversionistas y deja a las comunidades en condiciones vulnerables. Por ejemplo, el lenguaje de TPP establece en general que una medida adoptada por un Estado para proteger un objetivo de bienestar legítimo no debe ser considerada como expropiación excepto en raras circunstancias. Esta excepción y otras cuestiones relativas al poder regulador de un estado han creado varios debates. Este artículo recolecta estos debates y destaca el impacto del lenguaje del TPP en futuros tratados y acuerdos.

I. INTRODUCTION

The Trans-Pacific Partnership (the "TPP" or "the treaty") was signed on February 4, 2016. It was the end product of five years of negotiations between twelve countries and is the largest global trade agreement in the last twenty years.[2] Prior to the

---

[2] Once ratified, TPP would become the largest trade bloc on earth, concentrating forty percent of the world's gross domestic product. The signatories represent around 40 percent of the global economy and a quarter of world trade. Membership to the TPP is also open to other Asia-Pacific

expansion in 2016, the TPP was a regional free trade agreement between the United States, Canada, Australia, New Zealand, Japan, Singapore, Malaysia, Vietnam, Mexico, Chile, Peru and Brunei ("TPP Member States").[3] The TPP made history as the first ever mega-regional treaty to be concluded.[4] However, its ratification has been tainted by uncertainty after the United States Government signed an executive order to withdraw from TPP negotiations and the treaty overall.[5]

Notwithstanding the result of the TPP's negotiations, the language of the TPP set the basis for Bilateral Investment Treaty (BIT) and Free Trade Agreement reforms that are pending approval, ratification, and renegotiation.

Critics of the TPP, including experts in law and economics, have warned about the dangers of the Investor-State Dispute Settlement (ISDS) mechanism included in the TPP.[6] One major critique is that this mechanism impacts the sovereign rights of a State[7] and weakens the rule of law.[8] Critics contest that States'

---

countries, with both Republic of Korea and Indonesia expressing a strong interest in becoming signatories. *See* GITANJALI BAJAJ ET AL., DLA PIPER, THE TRANS-PACIFIC PARTNERSHIP SERIES: NAVIGATING A NEW ERA OF TRADE IN THE PACIFIC RIM: PART I – INVESTMENT PROTECTIONS & INVESTOR-STATE DISPUTE SETTLEMENT, 2 (2016), https://www.dlapiper.com/~/media/Files/Insights/Publications/2016/04/TPP%20Series_Part_1.pdf.

[3] *Id.* ("The signatories represent around 40 per cent of the global economy and a quarter of world trade. Membership to the TPP is also open to other Asia-Pacific countries, with both Korea and Indonesia expressing a strong interest in becoming signatories.").

[4] *See* PETER DRAPER ET AL., EUROPEAN CTR. FOR INT'L POLITICAL ECON., MEGA-REGIONAL TRADE AGREEMENTS: IMPLICATIONS FOR THE AFRICAN, CARIBBEAN, AND PACIFIC COUNTRIES 8, (2004), http://ecipe.org//app/uploads/2014/12/OCC22014.pdf (coining the term 'mega-regional).

[5] Presidential Memo, 82 Fed. Reg. 8497 (Jan. 23, 2017).

[6] 162 CONG. REC. S480 (daily ed. Feb. 2, 2016) (Statement of Senator Warren).

[7] Opponents to the TPP have argued that in general the ISDS system attacks the sovereignty of States because arbitral tribunals rather national courts analyze whether government measures fulfill international investment standards and consequently if such government can be found liable internationally.

[8] LAURENCE TRIBE ET AL., 220+ LAW AND ECONOMICS PROFESSORS URGE

sovereign rights are affected because States do not have freedom to adopt regulatory measures in certain circumstances under the Treaty. This is reflected in a recent trend of cases brought by investors, who have challenged States' regulatory measures passed in times of emergency, measures related to the use of natural resources, and public health measures, all of which include sensitive issues.[9]

Proponents posit that past experience has shown that ISDS is not a threat to a national government's regulatory power, as many critics claim. Out of the hundreds of resolved ISDS cases worldwide, few involved cases against legislative governmental actions, and cases that did challenge such sovereign actions, rarely succeeded.[10] The majority of measures that are challenged by investors involve breaches of administrative law, rather than general regulatory powers of States.

Central to the discussion by TPP critics is the treaty's language defending States' sovereign regulatory power. By incorporating language stating that regulatory actions should not be considered indirect expropriation, so long as they are designed and applied to protect legitimate public objectives, critics feel as though the TPP goes too far in protecting States' regulatory

---

CONGRESS TO REJECT THE TPP AND OTHER PROSPECTIVE DEALS THAT I=INCLUDE INVESTOR-STATE DISPUTE SETTLEMENT (ISDS), 2, (2016), https://www.citizen.org/sites/default/files/isds-law-economics-professors-letter-sept-2016.pdf; *see also* NIGEL CORY & STEPHEN EZELL, INFO. TECH. & INNOVATION FOUND., HOW TPP CRITICS MUDDLE FACTS, FICTIONS, AND UNFOUNDED FEARS: A POINT-BY-POINT ANALYSIS 15 (2016), http://www2.itif.org/2016-tpp-critics-muddle-facts-fiction.pdf?_ga=2.241631746.1268927901.1537972815-1923363078.1537823248. ("The most serious accusation leveled against ISDS are that it undermines state sovereignty, as it can overturn domestic court decisions and force a country to damage its laws – both of which are false. ISDS is not a threat to the core responsibilities of governments – it cannot be used to attack a country's health and social security systems, and regulations in the TPP explicitly confirm that every country retain the right to regulate in its public interest, including with regard to health, safety, the financial sector, and environment protection.").

[9] Philip Morris Brands Sàrl. v. Oriental Republic of Uruguay, ICSID Case No. ARB/10/7, Award (Jul. 8, 2016).

[10] Cory, *supra* note 8, at 16.

powers.[11] These contentious TPP provisions will be analyzed in the following sections.

II. Investment and Exception Chapters

The Investment and Exception chapters of the TPP contain language dealing with a State's regulatory power. The Investment Chapter of the TPP (Chapter Nine) offers investors a guideline that is considered to be the "Standard suite" of investment protections.[12] These provisions incorporate language such as *"rare circumstances"* and *"otherwise consistent with this chapter"* [13] to emphasize that regulatory measures adopted under a State power to regulate should not be considered an indirect expropriation, unless it meets such standards.[14] There are also several key provisions regarding investment protections in the TPP that host States must guarantee in order to fulfill the object and purpose of the treaty. These investment protections include, but are not limited to: National Treatment, Most-Favorable Nation Treatment, Minimum Standard of Treatment, and Expropriation and Compensation standards.

Additionally, the Exception Chapter of the TPP sets the language of the carve out clause regarding Tobacco Control.[15] Both chapters

---

[11] Regulatory measures regarding public health, safety and environment can be considered as a legitimate public objective that a State can adopt to protect its citizens.

[12] The TPP offers what can be thought of as the standard suite of protections for investors in the territory of the other Parties. These measures, which in the TPP generally govern both pre-establishment and post-establishments investments, include: National Treatment, Most Favoured Nation, Expropriation, Fair and Equitable Treatment, and more. *See* John W. Boscariol & Robert A. Glasgow, *Trans-Pacific Partnership—Investment Protection and Investor-State Claims*, McCarthy Tetrault (Nov. 26, 2015), https://www.mccarthy.ca/en/insights/blogs/terms-trade/trans-pacific-partnership-investment-protection-and-investor-state-claims.

[13] Trans-Pacific Partnership, art. 9.16, annex 9-B, Feb. 4, 2016, *never ratified*, https://ustr.gov/sites/default/files/TPP-Final-Text-Investment.pdf

[14] Such measures can be adopted in the context of public health, safety, environmental and other regulatory objectives.

[15] Trans-Pacific Partnership, *supra* note 13, art. 29.5,

language has been heavily criticized and left open to interpretation.

This article will highlight these criticisms and interpretations through three main considerations. The intention behind this article is to highlight positive aspects of the TPP's language dealing with State power to regulate and proposes that this language be used in future negotiations of BITs and Free Trade Agreements.

A. REGARDING "RARE CIRCUMSTANCES"

Article 9.8: Expropriation and Compensation in the TPP states that:

> 1. No Party shall expropriate or nationalize a covered investment either directly or indirectly through measures equivalent to expropriation or nationalization (expropriation), except:
> (a) for a public purpose;
> (b) in a non-discriminatory manner;
> (c) on payment of prompt, adequate and effective compensation in accordance with paragraphs 2, 3 and 4; and
> (d) in accordance with due process of law.[16]

This provision is similar to stipulations in other international investment agreements ("IIAs"). It protects a covered investment from both direct expropriation, the transfer of title or seizure of property,[17] and from indirect expropriation.[18] Indirect

---

https://ustr.gov/sites/default/files/TPP-Final-Text-Exceptions-and-General-Provisions.pdf.

[16] *Id.* art. 9.8, https://ustr.gov/sites/default/files/TPP-Final-Text-Investment.pdf.

[17] Mariana Pendás & Eduardo Mathison, *TPP and Investor-State Dispute Settlement: An Intertwined Spectrum of Options for Investors?*, 11 GLOBAL TRADE & CUSTOMS J. 157, 158 (2016).

[18] An action or series of actions by a TPP State Member that have an effect equivalent to direct expropriation without formal transfer of title or outright seizure. *See* GITANJALI BAJAJ ET AL., *supra* note 2, at 2 ("The signatories represent around 40 per cent of the global economy and a quarter of world trade. Membership to the TPP is also open to other Asia-Pacific countries, with both Korea and Indonesia expressing a strong interest in becoming

expropriation has become a defining characteristic of the right to regulate.[19] In this respect, investors should be aware that the TPP language provides certain limitations on the scope of an investments protection and was designed to preserve the freedom of TPP Member States to regulate in areas of public welfare, environment, and health.[20] This language was also incorporated into Annex 9-B 3(b) of the investment chapter as an additional source of Article 9.8 interpretation that regulates expropriation and compensation. This annex states that:

> "Non-discriminatory regulatory actions by a Party that are designed and applied to protect legitimate public welfare objectives, such as public health, safety and the environment, do not constitute indirect expropriations, *except in rare circumstances.*"[21] (emphasis added)

From a quick reading of this provision, it seems that State's sovereign right to adopt regulatory action to protect legitimate public welfare objectives should not be considered an indirect expropriation. However, the language "except in rare circumstances" opens the door to interpretation. Critics have focused on the words "rare circumstances" because the Investment

---

signatories.").

[19] CHRISTIAN TIETJE, FREYA RAETENS & ECORYS, MINISTER FOR FOREIGN TRADE & DEV. COOPERATION, THE IMPACT OF INVESTOR-STATE-DISPUTE SETTLEMENT (ISDS) IN THE TRANSATLANTIC TRADE AND INVESTMENT PARTNERSHIP 49 (2014), https://www.rijksoverheid.nl/binaries/rijksoverheid/documenten/rapporten/2014/06/24/the-impact-of-investor-state-dispute-settlement-isds-in-the-ttip/the-impact-of-investor-state-dispute-settlement-isds-in-the-ttip.pdf.

[20] Pendás & Mathison, *supra* note 17, at 158–159. ("Since 2004, IIA provisions have addressed the fear of States to provide them with the ability to regulate health, welfare and environment issues, and at the same time, the fear no to be impeded or punish with less investment.").

[21] Trans-Pacific Partnership, *supra* note 13, annex 9-B n.37 ("For greater certainty and without limiting the scope of this subparagraph, regulatory actions to protect public health include, among others, such measures with respect to the regulation, pricing and supply of, and reimbursement for, pharmaceuticals (including biological products), diagnostics, vaccines, medical devices, gene therapies and technologies, health-related aids and appliances and blood and blood-related products.").

Chapter of the TPP does not clarify the meaning of this standard.[22] In this regard, and because of a lack of guidance, a future international arbitral tribunal could interpret a regulation to be an indirect expropriation even when such the measure, in another context, could be adopted and applied to protect legitimate public welfare objectives.

It has been theorized that the language used in Annex 9-B, rather than be a safeguard, can act as a loophole to allow foreign corporations to challenge new State regulations, if such regulation diminished the value of the investor's operations.[23] Therefore, while the United State Trade Representative (USTR) touts this provision to be a safeguard, the ISDS tribunal has the power to decide which environmental or other public interest policies fall into the "rare circumstances" loophole.[24]

Even when there is no elaboration on when "rare circumstances" arise to render an otherwise non-compensable expropriation compensable, the absence of a regulatory expropriation in the applicable treaty does not foreclose States defending a taking as non-compensable,[25] or the investor from defending a taking as compensable.[26] In other words, if a treaty does

---

[22] Tsai-yu Lin, *Preventing Tobacco Companies' Interference with Tobacco Control Through Investor-State Dispute Settlement under the TPP*, 8 ASIAN J. WTO & INT'L HEALTH L. & POL'Y 565, 576 (2013).

[23] ILANA SOLOMON & BEN BEACHY, SIERRA CLUB, A DIRTY DEAL: HOW THE TRANS-PACIFIC PARTNERSHIP THREATENS OUR CLIMATE 7 (2015), https://content.sierraclub.org/creative-archive/sites/content.sierraclub.org.creative-archive/files/pdfs/1197%20Dirty%20Deals%20Report%20Web_03_low.pdf ("Some argue that the TPP's inclusion of this expansion foreign investor right could allow a foreign corporation, like BHP Billiton, for example, to challenge a new environmental regulation, such as additional permit requirement, as a TPP- prohibited "indirect expropriation" if it diminished the value of its fracking operations.").

[24] LAURENCE TRIBE ET AL., *supra* note 8, at 2.

[25] Jean Ho, *Investment Protection Under Succession Treaties* 32 ICSID Rev. Foreign Investment L.J. 59, 74 (2017).

[26] Les Laboratoires Servier, S.A.S. v. Republic of Poland, Case No. II SA.Wa 838/13, Award (Redacted), ¶¶ 582-584 (Feb. 14, 2012). ("Thus, the burden then falls onto the Claimants to show that Poland's regulatory actions were inconsistent with a legitimate exercise of Poland's police powers. If the

not establish in which rare circumstances a State's action can be compensable, the parties shall follow the general principle in international adjudication that "whoever asserts must prove". In order to do so, the party that asserts the claim must obtain and present the necessary evidence in order to prove its assertion.[27] The parties might also take into consideration that any interpretation they reach should be according to the object and purpose of the treaty.[28]

Independently of what side one may fall on, State or investor, by incorporating such language in the TPP, Member States have negotiated for this mandatory rule in order to protect their regulatory actions. There is a well-known phrase that "every rule has an exception," and this language "rare circumstances" might be one of them. It will be up to arbitral tribunals and the ability of a party's counsel to demonstrate that a specific State's regulatory action falls under such exception. In this respect, parties will play a crucial role in overcoming and giving meaning to this high standard of burden of proof.

B. REGARDING THE PROVISION "OTHERWISE CONSISTENT WITH THIS CHAPTER"

Article 9.16 "Investment and Environmental, Health and other Regulatory Objectives" is included in the Investment Chapter of the TPP. This article states:

> "Nothing in this Chapter shall be construed to prevent a Party from adopting, maintaining or enforcing *any measure otherwise consistent with this Chapter* that it

---

Claimants produce sufficient evidence for such a showing, the burden shifts to Poland to rebut it.").

[27] Azurix Corp. v. The Argentine Republic, ICSID Case No. ARB/01/12, Decision on the Application for Annulment of the Argentine Republic, ¶ 215 (Sept. 1, 2009). ("[T]he Committee considers the general principle in ICSID proceedings, and in international adjudication generally, to be that "who asserts must prove", and that in order to do so, the party which asserts must itself obtain and present the necessary evidence in order to prove what it asserts.")

[28] *See Investment*, OFFICE OF THE U.S. TRADE REPRESENTATIVE, https://ustr.gov/trade-agreements/free-trade-agreements/trans-pacific-partnership/tpp-chapter-chapter-negotiating-3 (last visited Sept. 26, 2016).

considers appropriate to ensure that investment activity in its territory is undertaken in a manner sensitive to environmental, health or other regulatory objectives." (Emphasis added)[29]

The language "otherwise consistent with this chapter" is essentially a window dressing. In essence, the provision states that a party can regulate however it chooses, as long as it does not violate other obligations stated in the investment chapter. While the language of the TPP might "underscore" countries' rights to regulate in the public interest, the treaty does not actually protect that right.[30] Instead, this article will likely provide only a slight interpretive gloss in favor of protecting public interest measures,[31] indicating to investors that such regulations are still able to be changed. For example, if good faith measures are taken in the public interest, they can still be successfully challenged under the agreement as violating the TPP's investor protections and thus negate any protections otherwise purported to be given under that article.[32]

Similarly, TPP Member States have the freedom to adopt measures appropriate to ensure that investment activity in their territories are undertaken in a manner sensitive to their environment, health or other regulatory objectives, provided that such measures are not otherwise inconsistent with the investment

---

[29] Trans-Pacific Partnership, *supra* note 13, art. 9.16, https://ustr.gov/sites/default/files/TPP-Final-Text-Investment.pdf.

[30] *See* Lise Johnson & Lisa Sachs, *The TPP's Investment Chapter: Entrenching, Rather than Reforming, a Flawed System*, Columbia Ctr. on Sustainable Inv. 2 (Nov. 2015), http://ccsi.columbia.edu/files/2015/11/TPP-entrenching-flaws-21-Nov-FINAL.pdf. ("That article [9.16] provides no such real protection. Rather, it simply notes that the government can regulate in the public interest as long as, when doing so, the government complies with the Investment Chapter's requirement regarding treatment of foreign investors and investments.").

[31] *Trading Views: Real Debates on Key Issues in TPP, Hearing on Trans Pacific Partnership Before the Subcomm. On Trade,* 114th Cong. (Dec. 2, 2015) (Statements of Ways and Means Democrats).

[32] Johnson & Sachs, *supra* note 30, at 2.

chapter.[33] In other words, Member States have the freedom to adopt regulations assuming that these measures do not otherwise constitute a breach of obligations set forth in the investment chapter. It is important to note here that TPP Member States have clearly used language favoring States' regulatory powers. In this respect, Article 9.16 expressly states that Member States have not only legitimacy to *adopt* regulatory actions recognized in article 9. 8, but also to *maintain* or *enforce* such measures to ensure that investment activity in its territory is undertaken in a manner sensitive to environmental, health, or other regulatory objectives.[34]

Nevertheless, a state that is going to exercise such regulatory power should not act arbitrarily or in violation of other obligations stated in the investment chapter, as is required by the language *"otherwise consistent with this chapter."* Therefore, in the context of the TPP and ISDS, State regulation should protect legitimate objectives in order to guarantee investor rights. Based on fairness, it cannot be justified to grant rights to one party (a State) and not another (an investor).

This provision of Article 9.16 ("otherwise consistent with this chapter") can help lawyers to improve their arguments during arbitration proceedings. In this regard, parties in a dispute must demonstrate that either the State respected its obligations when exercising its legitimate regulatory power, or that such regulatory power did not comport with the treaty's explicit obligations.

---

[33] The briefing also states that The TPPA's Chapter 9 (the Investment Chapter): (i) guarantees important protections to investments made by those nationals or companies; and (ii) contains investor-State dispute settlement (ISDS) provisions that entitle investors to submit disputes with TPP State Member to binding international arbitration. Much is the same as in other free trade and investment-protection agreements, but there are important differences requiring careful attention. *See Investment Protection and Investor-State Dispute Settlement under the Trans-Pacific Partnership Agreement* FRESHFIELDS BRUCKHAUS DERINGER (Nov. 17, 2015), http://knowledge.freshfields.com/en/Global/r/1325/investment_protection_a nd_investor-state_dispute.

[34] Trans-Pacific Partnership, *supra* note 13, art. 9.16, https://ustr.gov/sites/default/files/TPP-Final-Text-Investment.pdf.

C. The TPP Does Not Include Environment and Health Issues As Carve Outs.

Article 29.5 "Tobacco Control Measures" states that:

> "A Party may elect to *deny the benefits of Section B of Chapter 9 (Investment) with respect to claims challenging a tobacco control measure[35]* of the Party. Such a claim shall not be submitted to arbitration under Section B of Chapter 9 (Investment) if a Party has made such an election...." (Emphasis added)[36]

This article of the TPP embodies the carve-out clause of Tobacco Control Measures.[37] While the treaty has established filter mechanisms to avoid international claims[38] in other areas of public

---

[35] *Id.*, art. 29.5 n.12, https://ustr.gov/sites/default/files/TPP-Final-Text-Exceptions-and-General-Provisions.pdf ("A tobacco control measure means a measure of a Party related to the production or consumption of manufactured tobacco products (including products made or derived from tobacco), their distribution, labelling, packaging, advertising, marketing, promotion, sale, purchase, or use, as well as enforcement measures, such as inspection, recordkeeping, and reporting requirements. For greater certainty, a measure with respect to tobacco leaf that is not in the possession of a manufacturer of tobacco products or that is not part of a manufactured tobacco product is not a tobacco control measure.").

[36] *Id.* art. 29.5, https://ustr.gov/sites/default/files/TPP-Final-Text-Exceptions-and-General-Provisions.pdf.

[37] *Id.* It seems that this carve-out was formulated in response to the investment claim that a multinational Tobacco company brought against Australia to challenge the Tobacco Plain Packaging Bill (2011). *See also* Taejoon Ahn, The Utility of Carve-Out Clauses in Addressing Regulatory Concerns in Investment Treaty Arbitration 12 Asian Int'l Arb. J. 65, 72, 76 (2016) ("[T]o avoid regulatory concerns in certain regulatory areas, states need to carve out certain areas involving their vital regulatory concerns from the scope of international obligations in advance in the exercise of their sovereign choice. This is because just as the consent to international investment disciplines depends on a sovereign choice of each state, so the scope of the consent, namely the choice of certain areas included in the agreement and the exclusion of other areas from the agreement, is up to the sovereign state .... The carve-out clause is expected to be adopted by the new version of investment treaties as an effective instrument for alleviating regulatory concerns in terms of legal certainty, predictability and political acceptability.").

[38] Johnson & Sachs, *supra* note 30, at 3.

interest such as taxation measures[39] and financial services regulations, this does not mean that such regulations are not subject to conditions, such as the "exceptional circumstances" measure, included in Article 29.3 of the treaty.[40]

The fact that there are no filter mechanisms, as explained above, relating to environmental protection or public health issues in the TPP, has been criticized.[41] Authors have questioned why this clause is so narrow, applying only to tobacco measures, when governments deal with a much wider array of health and environmental issues which would merit exclusion from arbitration proceedings just as often.[42]

Other authors have used this carve-out clause to demonstrate that TPP Member States intentionally protected their regulatory power when public welfare objectives are at issue.[43] The will of TPP Member States is clear when public welfare objectives are

---

[39] Trans-Pacific Partnership, *supra* note 13, art. 29.4.9, https://ustr.gov/sites/default/files/TPP-Final-Text-Exceptions-and-General-Provisions.pdf ("Nothing in this Agreement shall prevent Singapore from adopting taxation measures no more trade restrictive than necessary to address Singapore's public policy objectives arising out of its specific constraints of space.").

[40] Mélida Hodgson, *The Trans-Pacific Partnership Investment Chapter Set a New Worldwide Standard* COLUMBIA FDI PERSPECTIVES 1 (Nov. 9 2015), https://academiccommons.columbia.edu/doi/10.7916/D86Q25WM/download ("Then there is a provision in the General Exceptions chapter allowing temporary financial safeguards in 'exceptional circumstances.' Clearly, the shadow of the Argentina investment jurisprudence looms large—various Asian-Pacific countries themselves had to deal with a scarring financial crisis around the same time."); *see also* Nahila Cortes, *Indirect Expropriation under the TPP: A New Frontier for the Right of States to Regulate?*, KLUWER ARBITRATION BLOG (Dec. 20 2015), http://arbitrationblog.kluwerarbitration.com/2015/12/20/indirect-expropriation-under-the-tpp-a-new-frontier-for-the-right-of-states-to-regulate/ ("Article 29.3 recognizes that the State may adopt or maintain restrictive temporary financial safeguards in exceptional circumstances if they are consistent with the TPP.").

[41] Johnson & Sachs, *supra* note 30, at 3.

[42] Nathalie Bernasconi-Osterwalder, *How the Investment Chapter of the Trans-Pacific Partnership Falls Short*, INT'L INST. FOR SUSTAINABLE DEV. BLOG (Nov. 6, 2015), https://www.iisd.org/blog/how-investment-chapter-trans-pacific-partnership-falls-short.

[43] GITANJALI BAJAJ ET AL., *supra* note 2, at 4.

involved, such as the regulation of tobacco packaging, which is that States should have more leeway and protections to regulate.[44]

The fact that tobacco control measures are continually used as examples of States' regulatory power to protect public health, and excluded from international claims, can be used as an analogy in future environmental cases. States could establish that environmental measures similar to tobacco control measures are adopted to protect their citizens' health, and should be excluded from international claims and considered as part of a State sovereign power to regulate. In general, both the tobacco and environmental State regulatory powers protect public welfare objectives. The question of why environmental, health, and other measures were not also incorporated as carve-outs in the TPP may not be solved in the near future. Without a doubt, the incorporation of tobacco control measures is a positive step in the development of the international investment regime. Continued discussion of these environmental and health issues will help to set new standards to be included as carve-outs in future BITs and other Free Trade Agreements.

CONCLUSION

One cannot deny the tremendous work that TPP's Member States have put in to incorporate standards that were the subject of criticism over the past few years, in particular the express incorporation of the State power to regulate based on legitimate public welfare objectives. The fact that this provision is included in the TPP progresses the development of the international investment arbitration regime and opens the doors for future discussions in the field. This article presents analysis of TPP treaty language and highlights the positive aspects of it, with the aim of encouraging the audience to consider the positive impacts of this language for future BITs and Free Trade Agreements.

---

[44] Luis Miguel Velarde Saffer & Amir Ardelan Farhadi, *ISDS in the TPP: Is the Recent Uproar in the US Merited?—Part II*, Kluwer Arb. Blog (Nov. 7 2016), http://arbitrationblog.kluwerarbitration.com/2016/11/07/isds-in-the-tpp-is-the-recent-uproar-in-the-us-merited-part-ii/.

The Restructuring Plan and the Role of Foreign Investments in the Italian System

Vito Cozzoli & Antonio Morelli

Introduction

Why should investors still be interested in Italy? With the collapse of some of the biggest Italian corporations, like Alitalia and Ilva, now is the time to rethink the role of foreign investments in the country. This Article seeks to demonstrate the suitability of regulations for establishing a restructuring plan, specifically targeting those regulations meant to harmonize market prerogatives with public interests during a time of economic crisis. In particular, this Article explores the interplay between corporate contingencies and the role of the public administration in the pursuit of a dynamic governance strategy for the Italian economic system using the inductive method.[1]

Recent reforms in the Italian insolvency regulatory framework, with ongoing amendments on restructuring plans, have created momentum for a reorganization of domestic corporate strategies vis-à-vis investor demands. Drawing lessons from the Italian experience, this Article challenges traditional ways of approaching bankruptcy proceedings and offers a contextually richer understanding the advantages to restructuring plans.

A restructuring plan in the Italian domestic legal system through a 'forward-looking' strategy aims to achieve a fresh start for debtors' business affairs. As a result, the advantages to undertake a restructuring plan is that an economic balance can be preserved through a less formal and more flexible tool as opposed to judicial intervention, which is typical in bankruptcy procedures. In this fashion, the restructuring plan could encourage broader state engagement in times of economic crisis, aiming to promptly and effectively address market prerogatives and public interests.

This study will shed light on the way the Italian business reorganization process is aimed at fostering growth and economic stability. Determining how a new legal framework could attract foreign investment is key to assessing success in the Italian model. In this respect, not only may restructuring plans serve as a basis for

---

[1] The inductive method represents a preferred theory in contemporary international law. *See* William Thomas Worster, *The Inductive and Deductive Methods in Customary Internationa lLaw Analysis: Traditional and Modern Approaches,* 45 GEO. J. INT'L L. 445 (2014). This method aims to garner inferences from particular events, acts, or phenomena in order to derive a general rule. Whether it is impossible to draw verdicts on the inferences that were ascertained, the validity of the conclusion lies on the quality of evidence used to support it. *See* John Vickers, *The Problem of Induction*§ 2, *in* STANFORD ENCYCLOPEDIA OF PHILOSOPHY (Edward N. Zalta ed., rev. ed. 2010), http://plato.stanford.edu/entries/induction-problem/. In order to provide adequate and genuine evidence, the Article takes into account emblematic cases of corporate contingencies with regard to the Italian economic system, in order to support the analysis on restructuring models.

economic revival, but also as a bulwark for social protection.

I. Background

A. Restructuring Plans: A 'Forward-looking' Model

Restructuring plans represent a concrete legal tool for public intervention in the economy. These plans not only aim at preserving the productive body of the corporation, but also ensure job security in order to promote economic equilibrium.[2] The management of the ongoing economic crisis would be best taken out through these 'forward-looking' models, which have two central goals. On one hand, such a model aims at promoting continuity in business activity through the attraction of foreign direct investment ("FDI"). On the other hand, it fosters built-in defenses for the domestic system through the recovery of production capacity and social protection, which ultimately support job security. As a result, forward-looking restructuring plans support national and international core business goals while also creating a fertile legal and administrative ground for foreign investors.

Restructuring is one strategy for corporations to avoid a total termination of their business, while also achieving economic continuity in the market. This is a public policy that aims to mitigate economic and social consequences, while negotiating different positions taken by investors and owners that hold company equity, as well as lenders and creditors who control debt. The rationale is to provide an effective and prompt solution to an emergency in the corporate condition.[3]

The restructuring process entails radical reforms in a

---

[2] *See* PATRICK A. GAUGHAN, MERGERS, ACQUISITIONS, AND CORPORATE RESTRUCTURINGS, 433 (6th ed., 2015) (analyzing restructuring plans in bankruptcy as a creative corporate finance tool, posing as an alternative to liquidation).

[3] Colin Anderson & David Morrison, *The Commencement of the Company Rescue: How and when does it start?*, *in* INTERNATIONAL INSOLVENCY LAW: THEMES AND PERSPECTIVES, 83, 83–85 (Paul J. Omar ed., 2008) (analyzing the rise of the so-called "rescue culture" and the determination of a rescue regime in insolvency procedure).

corporation's organization and structure in order to address serious financial and operational issues that could lead to shut down or liquidation. During this process, the organization's ownership changes and new contractual relationships are formed with creditors, debt holders, shareholders, employees, and other stakeholders. Ideally, restructuring will lead to the creation of businesses that are more likely to attract FDI with sound policy and regulatory framework supporting them. This ultimately revives the corporation to be a productive and profitable entity. Policymakers have struggled with large corporate business crises, as they hold an endemic risk tied to industry and large-scale unemployment. In other words, this is a public policy problem that needs to be addressed with appropriate legal tools, driven by flexibility and urgency.

Despite their relevance, restructuring plans have hardly been implemented through organic domestic regulation in response to a major corporate business crisis. Instead, such situations have historically been deferred to *ad hoc* laws for singular enterprises about to collapse. Both the rationale and effects of restructuring plans, with regard to 2007-8 global economic crisis, have rarely been the subject of research by international scholars. Within this framework, a "rescue culture" has emerged as demonstrated by the recent guidelines on insolvency authored by UNCITRAL and the World Bank.[4]

The traditional legal instruments that have dealt with business crises are grounded in bankruptcy law, which defers to the judiciary to determine the competence of the corporation's dismissal. Threats of another global economic crisis establish the need for different responses, as well as more effective and prompt solutions. In this

---

[4] *See* IAN F. FLETCHER, INSOLVENCY IN PRIVATE INTERNATIONAL LAW 500–503 (2d dd., 2005) (on the quest for international standards and principles in insolvency procedures, set out by the major international institutions, as UNCITRAL or the World Bank in 1999); *see also* TERENCE C. HALLIDAY & BRUCE G. CARRUTHERS, BANKRUPT: GLOBAL LAWMAKING AND SYSTEMIC FINANCIAL CRISIS 96–112 (2009) (analyzing the role of International Financial Institutions in developing a global regulation on bankruptcy for national insolvency systems).

light, domestic policymakers are resorting to new legal instruments like restructuring plans in order to provide corporate executives a stronger role and, in turn, with an augmented power of intervention in domestic markets. Indeed, since financial insolvencies trigger economic and social alarms, it is paramount for governmental authorities to provide quick and prompt answers at the disposal of large corporations.[5]

B. The 'Domino Effect'

The problem of the financial instability of large corporations is usually intertwined with cyclical economic crises. As a result, sovereign states have typically faced the issue of relying on *ad hoc* laws in order to intervene in a particular industry or for a particular corporation.[6] As the global financial crisis spread around the world, governments have grappled with the idea of establishing general regulations for corporate restructuring. Not only would a general domestic regulation further an economic purpose in the realm of public policy, but it would also tackle the social side effects embedded in the crisis.[7]

With public interests at stake, the intervention of government entities is necessary for complete economic recovery and the safeguarding of social values. In fact, contingencies of large corporations trigger significant repercussions, almost like a domino effect. The crisis generates an economic breakdown amplified with effects on all the ancillary activities and subsidiaries of such large multinational corporations.[8] Additionally, the crisis produces severe

---

[5] *See, e.g.*, Rodrigo Olivares-Caminal et al., Debt restructuring 36 (2011) (analyzing the legal framework of restructuring plans); *see also* Christine M. Cumming, *Managing Crises Without Government Guarantees: How Do We Get There?*, *in* OECD Journal: Financial Market Trends 2011, No. 2 (2012), 15-7 (analyzing the role of government in managing the financial crisis).

[6] *See* Fletcher, *supra* note 4, at 137–139 (on the evolution of insolvency regulation in private international law, from the sphere of natural persons to business corporations).

[7] *See* Gerard McCormack, Corporate rescue law: an Anglo-American perspective 209 (2008).

[8] *See* Jongho Kim, *Corporate Restructuring Through Spin-Off Reorganization Plan: A Korean Case Study*, 23 Pace Int'l L. Rev. 41, 43 (2011).

societal dilemmas, the most salient of which being unemployment.[9] Therefore, the countless consequences of large corporate crises are the issue motivating policy-makers find holistic economic and social policy solutions for these large-scale economic problems.[10]

C. Dichotomy Between Restructuring Plans and Bankruptcy Procedures

The distinction between bankruptcy procedures and restructuring plans lies within the rationale of each method. While the former is oriented to provide credit protection, the latter is focused on business continuity. For example, bankruptcy regulation is primarily based on credit protection and only through composition with creditors, it allows for the continuation of the business activity. Restructuring plans on the other hand, utilize economic and social safeguards with the expulsion of the executive management from the business entity, to help deliver a revitalized organization to new investors.[11] In this framework, analyzing the experience of the U.S. legal system, through the standards embedded in Chapter 7 and Chapter 11 of the United States Bankruptcy Code, may serve as an example to point out the main features and differences between bankruptcy procedures and restructuring plans.

Bankruptcy procedure is a legal mechanism purely based on liquidating the corporation in a solvency crisis. Interpretation of the meaning of crisis can range from temporary difficulties to a full state of insolvency. It aims to completely dismantle the enterprise, through the sale of its assets and with the consequent banishment of the corporation from the market. These procedures are designed to

---

[9] *See e.g.*, LAURA HORN, REGULATING CORPORATE GOVERNANCE IN THE EU: TOWARDS A MARKETIZATION OF CORPORATE CONTROL 168–69 (2012).

[10] *See* Anderson & Morrison, *supra* note 3, at 87–90 (analyzing the discipline of companies rescue through a comparative perspective, shedding light on the British, Australian, and American systems).

[11] *See* Daniel Hayek, Christina Meyer & Chantal Joris, *Restructuring over Liquidation*, 48 INT'L FIN. L. REV., 48, 48–51 (2015) (analyzing the dual choice between restructuring and liquidating corporations in distress).

seek protection for creditors.[12]

Bankruptcy agreements consist of a negotiation settlement, in which the decision to continue the business activity is not imposed by law, but is left to the parties involved to determine. In other words, the balance between liquidation and continuation is a private decision once the status of liability is settled. In the latter case, parties shall demonstrate that continuation is practical to the satisfaction of creditors.[13]

Regulation for restructuring plans take a completely different approach. For example, protection of the production system along with the continuity of business prevail over the interests of the creditors. Therefore, through a reconciliation of the interests at stake, the liquidation of corporate assets is mitigated with an eye towards market prerogatives and other public needs.

Restructuring plan regulations also have a special procedure in which domestic policymakers tend to balance the interests at stake while prioritizing the preservation of the business entity. To be found eligible under the restructuring plan regulations, the enterprise must be in a state of insolvency. In this situation, insolvency is defined as a non-transitory state in which the entrepreneur is unable to regularly fulfill corporate obligations.[14] Once the enterprise is found to be eligible, the plan can be activated through different scenarios; either as a result of the failure of private negotiations, or as a default provision. However, private agreements are not always sufficient to grant a business continuation of the

---

[12] Harry Rajak, *The Culture of Bankruptcy* 3, 17–25, *in* INTERNATIONAL INSOLVENCY LAW *supra* note 3 (analyzing bankruptcy regulation through a comparative perspective, describing the evolution of the British and the American systems).

[13] *See generally* GAUGHAN, *supra* note 2, at 433 (analyzing when bankruptcy is the best option); *see also* CHRISTOPHER A. WARD, ET AL., AMERICAN BANKRUPTCY INSTITUTE, THE CHIEF RESTRUCTURING OFFICER'S GUIDE TO BANKRUPTCY: VIEWS FROM LEADING INSOLVENCY PROFESSIONALS 10 (2013).

[14] LAWRENCE WESTBROOK, ET AL., A GLOBAL VIEW OF BUSINESS INSOLVENCY SYSTEMS 65 (2010) (analyzing liquidation procedures and the role of liquidators in domestic systems from a comparative perspective).

enterprise.[15]

In conclusion, external and internal considerations must be taken into account during large economic crises that negatively impact major business entities. If the business executives lose their legitimacy or credibility, or if they are no longer willing to continue managing the enterprise, then it is the role of the country's regulatory system to intervene through a restructuring plan to protect the public interests at stake. In other words, restructuring regulations are a set of domestic policies that preserve productivity and employment stability, while maintaining the balance between the interests of all the relevant stakeholders, not solely creditors.[16] The framework created thus far demonstrates how restructuring plans can re-establish the economic balance of corporations in crisis, and how tailored regulatory frameworks can attract FDI into domestic systems.

II. Analysis

A. The Italian System

The regulation of restructuring plans has a long tradition in the Italian system, where it has been regulated for nearly forty years with different models being adopted over that time period. In recent times, such regulation caught the attention of investors worldwide, as the financial crisis triggered new challenges for the Italian economic system.[17] The cases of ILVA and Alitalia, considered amongst the largest domestic Italian corporations, demonstrate the

---

[15] See MCCORMACK supra note 7, at 251.

[16] See MARK S. SCARBERRY ET AL., BUSINESS REORGANIZATION IN BANKRUPTCY: CASES AND MATERIALS 812 (4th ed., 2012).

[17] See Tiziana Del Prete & Matteo Smacchi, Italy, in THE RESTRUCTURING REVIEW, 152, 152 (Cristopher Mallon ed., 7th ed., 2014); see e.g., Stefania Pacchi Pescucci, L'amministrazoine Straordinaria delle Imprese di Rilevanti Dimensioni [Restructuring Plans of Large Corporations], in TRATTATO DI DIRITTO DELLE PROCEDURE CONCORSUALI, 833, 833 (U. Apice ed., 2011); see also Vittorio Zanichelli, L'amministrazione Straordinaria [The Restructuring Plans], in FALLIMENTO E ALTRE PROCEDURE CONCORSUALI, 2010, 2074 (Giuseppe Fauceglia & Luciano Panzani, eds., 2009).

need for an effective policy and regulatory framework on restructuring plans. After analyzing the evolution of the Italian system, this Article will focus on current reforms, which are deemed necessary to create a sound framework for attracting FDI into Italy.

B. The Italian Regulatory Framework

In 1979, the Italian Parliament introduced for the first time a regulation on business crises of large corporations.[18] In order to make it compatible with the European Union framework on competition law in the late 1990s, the regulation underwent a revision process. On June 17, 1999 the European Court of Justice found the Italian law incompatible with European standards and specifically, with the regime on competition and state aid.[19] The EU system does not allow automatic state aid, especially without any sort of distinction between meritorious and unworthy enterprises.

Following the Court's ruling on compliance with the EU legal framework on competition, Italy further revised the regulatory system with Legislative Decree no. 270 in 1999.[20] This was the so-called "Prodi" procedure, named after Minister Romano Prodi. With this reform, Italy opted for a model that required reliance on the judiciary to administer the plan.[21] Italian courts were then pressed to decide, whether the application of the Prodi procedure was compliant with the already existing restructuring regulatory system. The Italian Constitutional Court affirmed that the new procedure was compliant and that governmental authorities should both implement and manage the restructuring plan.[22]

---

[18] The first regulation on restructuring plans for large enterprises was adopted with the Law Decree 30 January 1979, n. 26 – converted with modifications into the Law no. 953 of 3 April 1979. *See* Decreto Legge 3 aprile 1979, n.95, G.U. Apr. 4, 1979, n.94 (It.).

[19] Case C-295/97, Industrie Aeronautiche e Meccaniche Rinaldo Piaggio SpA v. International Factors Italia SpA, 1999 E.C.R. I-03735.

[20] D.L. n.94/1979 (It.).

[21] *See* Steffen Koch, *Restructuring: The German Approach*, 3 INSOLVENCY & RESTRUCTURING INT'L, 27, 28 (2009) (analyzing the judiciary-based model, also with regard to its application in the German system).

[22] The Italian Constitutional Court analyzed the compliance of the procedure of the Law Decree n.26/1979 under the standards of the Italian Constitution. *See*

According to the restructuring regulation, only three classes of actors are authorized to initiate such procedures, including: the business' executives; one or more creditors of the enterprise; or the public prosecutor, *ex oficio*.[23] Once the request to restructure is received, the Court issues a decision to declare the state of insolvency. The Court then appoints a judicial committee, determining whether the management of the enterprise should be left to the insolvent entrepreneur or entrusted to the latter body – composed of either one or three commissioners – previously designated by the Ministry of Economic Development. [24]

After declaring a state of insolvency, the Court opens an observation period, which consists of two different phases: First, there is a period of 30 days granted to the judicial commission; then, there is another period of 30 days for the Court to decide whether the situation is ripe to begin the restructuring plan, based on the opinion of the Ministry of Economic Development and observations presented by creditors.[25]

In its report, the judicial committee indicates the causes of the state of insolvency and expresses, with reasoned assessment, that either current conditions support the implementation of a restructuring plan or do not. The report carries out a prognosis of the situation and methods for recovering the economic balance of the business activity. Moreover, the document includes an analysis and estimate of the corporation's assets, a list of creditors, and an

---

Corte Cost., 11 novembre 1987, n. 401; *see also* Corte Cost., 20 dicembre 1982, n. 244 (as the Court stated, compliance of the regulation with restructuring plans is grounded in the rationale of rehabilitation, which is of paramount interest to all relevant stakeholders, including creditors).

[23] Decreto Legislativo 8 luglio 1999, n.270, art. 2, G.U Aug. 9, 1999, n.185 (It.) (regulating the procedure for invoking restructuring plan in the Italian system).

[24] *See* Giorgio Oppo, *Profilo Sistematico dell'Amministrazione Straordinaria delle Grandi Imprese in Crisi* [System Profiles of Restructuring Plans of Large Corporations in Crisis], *in* VIRIVISTA DI DIRITTO CIVILE, 233 *et seq.* (1981) (discussion about the procedural aspects of the regulation).

[25] *See* Renato Rordorf, *Le Procedure Concorsuali e la «Par condicio» fra Diritto Positivo, Usi Alternativi e Prospettive di Riforma*, LA TUTELA DEI DIRITTI SOGGETTIVI NELLE PROCEDURE CONCORSUALI, QUADERNI DEL C.S.M., n.25, 15 *et seq.* (1989).

indication of their respective interests. This preliminary procedure gives grounds for the Court to formulate its own assessments regarding the measure to be implemented.[26]

The Court, after analyzing the report of the judicial committee, has two options.[27] Given suggestions to recover the economic balance, the Court could start the restructuring plan of the business entity; otherwise, it could issue a bankruptcy decree.

If the Court decides to establish a restructuring procedure, then government agencies were authorized to take action. The Ministry of Economic Development, within five days, appoints an extraordinary committee composed by one or three Commissioners,[28] typically constituted of the same individuals who had already served as judicial commissioner.[29]

In 2003, the Italian parliament passed a reform to the "Prodi" procedure, moving to an executive-managed model. The so-called "Marzano" procedure, named after the proposing Minister Antonio Marzano, established "urgent measures for industrial restructuring of large enterprises in crisis in order to intervene in a concrete case of emergency.[30] This reform was initiated in response to problems within the Italian agricultural industry, as swift public intervention was needed. [31]

---

[26] *See e.g.* Pescucci, *supra* note 17.

[27] D. Lgs. n. 270/1999, arts. 27–30 (regulating procedural aspects and the role the Judiciary plays in it, authorizing restructuring plans).

[28] *Id.* art. 38 (regulating the composition and tasks of the extraordinary committee).

[29] *See* Giorgio Marinucci, *La nuova disciplina dell'amministrazione straordinaria delle grandi imprese in stato di insolvenza* [The New Regulation on Restructuring Plans of Large Corporations in State of Insolvency], Commentary to D. Lgs. n.270/1999, 299 (Angelo Castagnola & Roberto Sacchi eds., 2000).

[30] Decreto Legge 23 dicembre 2003, n.347, Dec. 24, 2003, G.U. n.298 (It.).

[31] *See generally* Stefano Ambrosini, *Fallimento, Soluzioni Negoziate della Crisi e Disciplina Bancaria dopo le riforme del 2015 e 2016* [Insolvency, Negotiated Solutions of Crisis and Banking Discipline after 2015 and 2016 Reforms], in STRUMENTI DEL DIRITTO FALLIMENTARE, 779 (A. Signorelli ed., 2017).

This new model incorporated the need for swift and timely interventions. Under this reform, executive authorities, following a request to public authorities, could now autonomously decide whether the conditions for the restructuring plan are met and how to deal with the crisis. Shifting away from the prior model, the Italian parliament designed a relevant role for government to play in such plan. Under this framework, the Ministry of Economic Development was entrusted as a third and impartial authority to the manage the procedure. Indeed, government intervention seemed to better suit the challenges faced by large corporations, where social and economic principles are more centrally at stake.[32]

Under the Marzano reform, judicial administration is set aside from the procedure for three reasons. First, managing business crises does not fall under the Italian judiciary's mandate. Second, the judiciary lacks the adequate tools for crisis management as the length of judicial procedures do not correspond well with the need to achieve a swift resolution and appreciation of social interests, for which public administration may better serve. Third, only the government has the instruments to promote industrial restructuring and conversion processes.[33]

Pursuant to this new reform on restructuring, state intervention in crisis management is tailored to the impact that the crisis has in the public sector. Thus, the greater the impact is, the quicker the intervention should be. With a reasonable pleading and appropriate documentation, corporations dealing with financial emergencies may request the Court for insolvency status and the Ministry of Economic Development for the immediate admission to the

---

[32] See ROBERTO MARRAFFA, AMMINISTRAZIONE STRAORDINARIA DELLE GRANDI IMPRESE IN CRISI E TUTELA DEI CREDITORI [RESTRUCTURING PLANS OF LARGE CORPORATIONS IN CRISIS AND CREDITORS' PROTECTION] 6–7 (2012) (analyzing the role of the government in the procedure); see generally Luca Ponti & Francesca Spadetto, L'amministrazione Straordinaria Delle Grandi Imprese In Crisi [Restructuring Plans of Large Corporations] (2006) (highlighting the need for alternative insolvency procedures to bankruptcy for large corporations).
[33] See Fabrizio Di Marzo & Francesco Macario, Amministrazione Straordinaria delle Grandi Imprese in Stato di Insolvenza [Restructuring Plans of Large Corporations in Insolvency Status], in TRATTATO DELLE PROCEDURE CONCORSUALI, 601 (A. Jorio, B.N. Sassani eds., 2017).

restructuring plan. In order to identify the subjects eligible for restructuring plans, current Italian procedures set out two requirements based on employment features and patrimonial structure.[34] First, the corporation shall have more than two hundred subordinate employees for at least one year. Second, it holds total amount of debts in the amount of two-thirds or more of both total assets and revenues from sales and services in the previous financial year. In the case of a holding company, the activation of a restructuring plan does not extend to the entity's other companies. Conditions for access to the restructuring plan for a complete holding company are determined in the prospects for recovering economic balance, or the opportunity to successfully manage the insolvency of the group.[35] Nonetheless, once the Ministry of Economic Development receives a pleading a holding company, it retains the authority to directly admit the holding company to the restructuring plan.

Designing the restructuring plan is a task given to the same committee appointed by the Ministry of Economic Development, under the supervision of the Ministry itself. This operation must be tailored to comply with domestic industrial policy guidelines, in order to safeguard the unity of business entities, while also taking the interests of creditors into account. Within 60 days from the first decree, the committee submits a final draft of the restructuring plan to the Ministry of Economic Development.[36] Within 15 days from the executive decree, the Court declares the insolvency status of the corporation.

Throughout the execution of the plan, dialogue between the committee and the Ministry is maintained through regular reports on the business performance of the corporation submitted every three

---

[34] D.L. n.347/2003, art. 2 (It.) (identifying the subjects eligible for restructuring plans).

[35] See Nicolò Baccetti, *Requisiti per l'ammissione* [*Requirements for Admission*], *in* LA LEGGE MARZANO, COMMENTARIO, 1–45 (Angelo Castagnola & Roberto Sacchi eds., 2006) (analyzing the prospects of recovering as a requirement for the procedure).

[36] D.L. n. 347/2003, art. 54 (It.) ((defining the procedural requirements necessary to issue a restructuring plan).

months, including a status of implementation of the program. During this time, the committee is entitled to take control of the enterprise's management by administering corporate assets.[37] Eventually, at the end of the procedure, a final report indicates whether the objectives were met, or whether the procedure failed. If, over the course of the implementation period, the restructuring plan is found to no longer be effectively applied, the committee can request the Court to convert the restructuring plan into a bankruptcy procedure.

C. Case Studies: ILVA and Alitalia

This analysis will now shed light on the state of emergency for two major Italian corporations, ILVA and Alitalia. Considered to be economic backbones for the national economic system, these corporations serve as empirical studies to benchmark the role of restructuring plans moving forward.

ILVA is a large Italian corporation with a long standing tradition in the steel sector.[38] Founded in 1905, it helped guide Italy through its industrialization process. Today, the corporation has more than twelve thousand employees, with its main office in Taranto. Since 2015, ILVA has been undergoing a restructuring plan pursuant to the Marzano procedure.[39] The plan encompassed the whole group of ILVA, including subsidiaries in order to reorder and re-launch the industrial potential of the corporation. In line with the purpose of the restructuring regime, the plan has three main goals. First, it aims to safeguard productivity. Since ILVA has a productive structure with several braches across Italy, the restructuring plan seems to be a sound strategy for both local prosperity and the stability of the national economy. Second, it aims to deliver a solid and reliable result that will ensure business prosperity and sustainable growth into the future. Third, it seeks to create a strategic

---

[37] *Id.* art. 40 (delimiting the competence of the committee).

[38] ILVA GROUP, http://www.gruppoilva.com/en (last visited Sept. 27, 2018).

[39] With the Ministerial Decree of 21 January 2015, ILVA s.p.a. has entered restructuring plan procedures for shifting corporate management under the control of an extraordinary committee, pursuant to the Law Decree no. 347, 2003. *See* Decreto Ministeriale 21 gennaio 2015 *pursuant to* D.L. n.347/2003. *See also supra* IIIA.

role for ILVA, not only at the national level, but also in international markets, so that it can interact with foreign partners and attract foreign investors.[40]

The ILVA restructuring plan resulted in an acquisition proposal issued by AM Investco Italy, a joint venture represented by 85% ArcelorMittal and 15% Marcegaglia Group. Following the proposal, and after hearing relevant stakeholders involved in the process on June 5, 2017, the Ministry of Economic Development signed a decree to start adjudication for the ILVA industrial complex.[41] The EU Commission is scrutinizing the validity of this decision under the EU standards on competition law, and it will presumably issue a decision by October 26, 2017.[42]

Established in 1947, Alitalia has more than eleven thousand employees, therefore meeting the requirements to be considered a large corporation under Italian legislation. The company has been going through a long-term financial crisis since 2008, spanning two different regimes of ownership.[43] With continued losses in Spring 2017, the corporation attempted to negotiate an agreement for business recapitalization between the corporate management board and trade unions. Nonetheless, an internal referendum held on April

---

[40] *Extraordinary Administration*, ILVA GROUP,
http://www.gruppoilva.com/en/governance/governance/extraordinary-administration (last visited Sept. 27, 2018).

[41] *See Firmato il decreto di aggiudicazione del complesso industriale del Gruppo Ilva ad Am Investco Italy*, MINISTRY OF ECON. DEV. (Jun. 5, 2017), http://www.sviluppoeconomico.gov.it/index.php/it/per-i-media/comunicati-stampa/2036649-calenda-firma-il-decreto-di-aggiudicazione-del-complesso-industriale-del-gruppo-ilva-ad-am-investco-italy.

[42] *See* Matteo Menghello, *Ilva, contatti Mittal-Arvedi bussa in vista del verdetto dell'antitrust europeo*, IL SOLE 24 ORE (Sept. 23, 2017) http://www.ilsole24ore.com/art/impresa-e-territori/2017-09-23/ilva-arvedi-bussa-vista-un-no-dell-antitrust--184620.shtml?uuid=AEjYKeYC&refresh_ce=1.

[43] Alitalia was first acquired by CAI (Compagnia Aerea Italiana) Group in 2009, and then in 2015 it started a joint venture with Etihad Airways, where the latter holds 49% of corporate capital. *See Alitalia*, AIRLINEFILES.COMhttp://airlinefiles.com/alitalia?showall=1&limitstart= (last visited Sept. 27, 2018).

25, 2017 rejected this agreement.[44] As a result of the referendum, and given the financial distress of the corporation, on May 2, 2017 the board filed a request to the Government for a restructuring plan.[45] The Ministry for Economic Development, pursuant to the Marzano procedure, appointed an *ad hoc* committee for the corporation to carry out interim management.[46] Since the Government excluded *a priori* in its declarations, the opportunity to nationalize the company through a public bid process, the committee has been working on a new plan to reposition the corporation in domestic and international markets.[47]

Restructuring plans are necessary for cases like ILVA and Alitalia, two pillars of the Italian economic system. The Government's decision to initiate the plans not only aims to safeguard corporations amongst the largest in the Italian economy, but also to avoid systemic economic risk. Considering the scale of their operations, downward economic and social effects would impact the country not only at the local level, but also on a national scale. In this respect, undergoing a restructuring plan with the intent of attracting FDI may represent a fresh start for these debtors' business affairs. It is therefore essential that Italy secures a legal and administrative framework to establish a fertile ground for foreign investors in respect to these two companies. To this end, the opportunity for reformation of the current restructuring plan regulations is particularly timely and necessary.

D. The Opportunity for Reform and Future Scenarios

Italian policymakers are currently discussing a reform on

---

[44] *See* Giorgio Pogliotti, *Referendum Alitalia, vince il «no»*, IL SOLE 24 ORE (Apr. 25, 2017) http://www.ilsole24ore.com/art/notizie/2017-04-24/referendum-alitalia-vince-no-230012.shtml.

[45] *Comunicato Stampa 2 maggio 2017*, ALITALIA (May 2, 2017), http://corporate.alitalia.it/it/media/comunicati-sai/2017-05-02.html.

[46] Decreto 2 maggio 2017, G.U. May 6, 2017, n.104 (It.) *pursuant to* D.L. n. 347/2003 (It.).

[47] *See* Giorgio Pogliotti, *Alitalia, i Commissari: oltre 600 milioni ancora disponibili*, IL SOLE 24 ORE (Jun. 14, 2017), http://www.ilsole24ore.com/art/notizie/2017-06-14/alitalia-commissari-oltre-600-milioni-ancora-disponibili--173420.shtml?uuid=AEuSnYeB&refresh_ce=1.

domestic insolvency procedures within the parliament. The Ministry of Justice's commission, established in 2015 by executive decree, was tasked to create proposals for amendments to the current regulation for insolvency procedures. The Ministry of Justice, through its relevant subcommittees and in coordination with the Ministry of Economic Development, aims to provide an organic framework that harmonizes the judiciary's needs with administrative prerogatives in restructuring plans for large corporations in crisis.[48]

The reform integrates provisions contained in Legislative Decree no. 270/1999, or the Prodi procedure, with those embedded in Law Decree n. 347/2003 and subsequent amendments, or the Marzano procedure, for possible regulatory improvements.[49] Based on the principle of transparency, these procedures promote independence and integrity.

The goal is to create a harmonized regulatory framework that is able to foster the revitalization of troubled businesses and solve financial crises for Italian corporations. The subject matter of the reform is limited to large corporations, in order to prevent systemic risks in the domestic economy.

Reforms to the restructuring regulations include procedural steps like structural requirements for corporations to be admitted to a restructuring plan, and the criteria for the appointment of the extraordinary committee. It harmonizes domestic regulation within the EU framework to comply with the EU Commission Recommendation 2003/361/EC set forth on May 6, 2003 which the defined micro, small, and medium sized enterprises, and also raises the minimum number of employees for the corporation to be eligible

---

[48] See Luciano Panzani, *Conservazione dell'impresa, interesse pubblico e tutela dei creditori: considerazioni a margine della Proposta di direttiva in tema di armonizzazione delle procedure di ristrutturazione* [*Conservation of the Business, of Public Interest and Creditors' Protection: Considerations as a Result of the Proposal for a Directive on Harmonization of Restructuring Procedures*], CRISI D'IMPRESA E FALLIMENTO (Sept. 11, 2017), http://blog.ilcaso.it/libreriaFile/977.pdf.

[49] *See* Del Prete & Smacchi, *supra*, note 17.

for the plan from 200 to 250.[50] Current quantitative requirements related to the number of employees and the volume of revenues and assets, should not be replaced by qualitative parameters related to the strategic relevance of the corporation within the framework of the national economic system. In this light, the regulation is designed to comply with the EU system and, in particular, with the provisions on competition and state aid.

State aid, pursuant to the meaning of Article 107 (1) of the Treaty for the Functioning of the European Union, is meant to favor certain businesses or certain industries. This framework risks distorting or threatening EU competition while also affecting trade between Member States.[51] As a result, restructuring plans may fall under the restrictions of state aid regulations, as far as it would allow a selective advantage to certain corporations or economic sectors to remain profitable in the market, solely based on a discretionary provision.[52]

The current reform is tailored to adjust Italian restructuring regulation to comply with the the EU framework on competition law. In order to maintain a balanced economic and social framework in the domestic system, and in compliance with the EU system, only cases of relevant downward economic effects of corporate crisis may public intervention be initiated.

This means that the corporation entrusts the government with the authority of corporate management. As an impartial actor, the government is tasked with returning a solid and reliable business

---

[50] Commission Recommendation of 6 May 2003, U.N. Doc. 2003/361/EC (May 6, 2003) (recommending that a medium company has less than 250 employees, with an annual turnover that does not exceed 50 million euros and a total annual budget that does not exceed 43 million euros).

[51] *See* Nikolaos E. Farantouris, *EU Competition Policy on State Aid for Rescuing and Restructuring Companies, in* THE REFORM OF EC COMPETITION LAW: NEW CHALLENGES (Ioannis Lianos & Ioannis Kokkoris eds., 2010) (analyzing EU competition standards in light of restructuring legal framework in the common market).

[52] *See* Case C-295/97, Industrie Aeronautiche e Meccaniche Rinaldo Piaggio SpA v. International Factors Italia SpA, 1999 E.C.R. I-03735; *see also* Case C-200-97, Ecotrade Srl v. Altiforni e Ferriere di Servola SpA, 1998 E.C.R. I-7907.

entity back to the market, cleansed from previous irresponsibility. On the other hand, it also creates a sound administrative and legal environment to allow FDI to enter and thrive in the domestic system.

Rather than having a system based on *ad hoc* laws to provide urgent solutions to individual cases, the Italian parliament is seeking to establish an organic legal and administrative framework for restructuring plans. With an *ex ante* regulation that is in compliance with EU competition standards, it will provide an effective and updated tool to address large corporate crises in the future.

Given the persistence of the financial crisis, Italian policymakers are essential to prevent large corporate crises from having a collateral impact on Italian society. These reforms seek to establish a faster approach to make the current restructuring plan procedures more transparent and less onerous for the corporations.

CONCLUSION

Since most of the economies affected by the global financial crisis are struggling in restarting growth, structural and institutional reforms are key for the achievement of macroeconomic stability. Restructuring plans have been enacted in economies facing crisis in order to encourage and protect foreign investments. Some countries, like Italy and the U.S., have adopted revised foreign investment laws that offer investors essential guarantees and protections. Based on a program that not only guarantees business continuity, but also safeguards employment rates, restructuring plans aim at returning corporations in crisis to profitability for domestic economic stability. These plans provide foreign investors with a just and equal legal regime, as well as continuous protection. Moreover, restructuring plans are tailored to transform a previously struggling economic entity into a solid, reliable, and safe entity cleansed from its previous debts. Consequently, efforts to improve legislation on foreign investments and current restructuring plans are oriented toward the creation of a legal regime that is consistent with international standards on competition and transparency.

www.ingramcontent.com/pod-product-compliance
Lightning Source LLC
Chambersburg PA
CBHW072016230526
45468CB00021B/1622